LIVING IN THE SPIRIT
Is It Real?

LIVING
IN THE SPIRIT
Is It Real?

by

Manford George Gutzke

BAKER BOOK HOUSE
Grand Rapids, Michigan

First printing, May 1972
Second printing, March 1973
ISBN: 0-8010-3662-3

Printed in the United States of America

Contents

LIVING IN THE SPIRIT
Is It Real?

1.

Two Worlds

Do you realize that a Christian lives in two worlds? A Christian thinks differently than the natural man, and this is not because he has better logic or because he has better morals or because he has better ethics. All of that may be true, but that would be true also for people that aren't Christians. The Christian believes not only in this world: he believes both in this world and in another world. In his body the Christian lives in this natural world like everyone else on earth, dealing with things by his physical senses; in his spirit he lives in the other world—the world of the spirit by faith, by the Word of God. This world is where human beings live, commonly called Earth; that other world is where God is, commonly called Heaven. The other world is discussed for us in I Corinthians 15:39-50.

> All flesh is not the same flesh: but there is one kind of flesh of men, another flesh of beasts, another of fishes, and another of birds. There are also celestial bodies, and bodies terrestrial: but the glory of the celestial is one, and the glory of the terrestrial is another. There is one glory of the sun, and another glory of the moon, and another glory of the stars: for one star differeth from another star in glory. So also is the resurrection of the dead. It is sown in corruption; it is raised in incorruption: it is sown in dishonor; it is raised in glory: it is sown in weakness; it is raised in power: it is sown a natural body; it is raised a spiritual body. There is a natural body, and there is a spiritual body. And so it is written, The first man Adam was made a living soul; the last Adam was made a quickening spirit. Howbeit that was not first which is spiritual, but that which is natural; and afterward that which is spiritual. The first man is of the earth, earthy: the second man is the Lord from heaven.

> As is the earthy, such are they also that are earthy: and as is the heavenly, such are they also that are heavenly. And as we have borne the image of the earthy, we shall also bear the image of the heavenly. Now this I say, brethren, that flesh and blood cannot inherit the kingdom of God; neither doth corruption inherit incorruption.

Paul was contrasting two different kinds of living and of being, commonly indicated by the words, earth and heaven. Christians are related to each of them: they are related to the things on earth by sight, and they are related to the things in heaven by faith.

It is the consensus of men everywhere that there is more to a man than his body. Even among people who are not Christians, there is a widespread belief in spirits. It is hard to conceive a person that doesn't have a body, a person who is spiritual and is invisible. Such a person would be intangible, he could not be touched, he would be inaudible, he could not be heard. It is no wonder that so many would find this incredible. Yet so much of all that matters to a Christian is involved in this whole truth; it is so very important.

In order to understand something of what this means, let us consider a person like your mother. Could anyone tell you that there's nothing more to your mother than her body? When you have bones and the muscles and the nerves, you have your mother. Is that all? And when that body ceases functioning, do you mean everything is obliterated, wiped out? Or consider your husband, your wife, your friend, or, if you're in love, your beloved: could you accept the idea there's nothing more to that person than the physical body? Or consider a baby lying in its crib, could you be satisfied to think there's nothing more there than a gathering together of certain atoms in such a way as to make bones and muscles and nerves, causing this organism to exist in this way?

This line of reasoning is even more important when we think about God. God, so far as we know, does not have a body such as we have. We speak of Him as being invisible. My own personal interest in this whole line of truth began in my interest in my mother. I didn't think of this at the time she died, when I was three-and-a-half years old. But later when I was still a boy I began to wonder, Is my mother alive? Will I ever see her? Will I ever be with her in fellowship? That raised another question, Is heaven real? And that raised another question, Is there such a being as God? I could understand if there is God, there could be heaven; and if there could be a heaven then my mother might be in it; and I might even get to be there if I was acceptable to God. But I had never seen God and no human being had ever seen God: then how could I believe in God? And why should I believe in God?

These questions arise right at this very point when we're thinking about the other world: Is there a God? Is there a heaven? Is there a soul? Is there anything real that you cannot see? Can I believe in the reality of anything that I have never seen? Consider this: I've never seen Europe, but I feel sure it's there. I've never seen Paris, but I think it's there. Can I believe it? Yes, I can believe it, and you could tell me: "Of course, you can believe it." And I'll ask, "Why, of course?" You will say, "You've got evidence." And right here is the crux of the matter. It is true I've never seen Napoleon: but I think he lived. I never saw Julius Caesar; but I think he lived. Can I believe those men lived? Yes, I can believe it. You'll say to me, "Of course, you can, because you've got evidence." This is exactly the point. Because I have evidence I can believe.

By the way, I've never seen flying horses. They are talked about in mythology, and there have been pictures of them drawn in the past by certain artists, but I've never seen one, nor has anyone else. I've never seen a mermaid, half-woman and half-fish. I've never seen anything like that. Could I believe such to be real? So far as I have heard, no one has ever seen one. Then, can I believe it? No! I cannot believe it. If I have evidence I can believe it. If I do not have evidence I cannot believe it. I've never seen little Red Riding Hood, and you know I don't believe she is real. I know the story, but I don't know of anyone who claims to have seen her. With no supporting evidence, I cannot believe.

Can I ever believe anything I have not seen? Upon the basis of supporting reason: when it is intelligent to believe, I can believe. For instance, you may never have seen my father. Do you think I had one? Yes, you believe that. You never saw him, but you believe it. Why? Because that is reasonable. Consider if there is a picture hanging on the wall, can you believe there was an artist? Or would you think that picture just happened? If you see a machine, can you believe there is a mechanic? Or would you think that machine just fell together? The matter of believing in the invisible God is just that reasonable.

What do Christians basically affirm about God? They don't describe Him; they say, "I believe in God the Father Almighty, Maker of heaven and earth." They mean He is Creator of all that is. Christians tell the whole world: "The heavens declare the glory of God; the firmament showeth his handiwork." They urge anyone: "Go out and look at the stars. Lift up your face and look into the sky. That's what God made and behind that, over that, beyond that, is where God is." That is reasonable and it can be believed.

In the case of any human being there is more than the body. Consider a man who has had an accident and has lost both legs, is he still a man? Yes! Is he the same man? Yes! Was he Tom Brown? Yes! Is he now Tom Brown? Yes, he is! Same man! Not as much of his body, but the same person. I can believe that you are you, even though I cannot see the "you" inside your body or apart from your body. Our conviction about God is based partly on our inward feeling about ourselves. We feel sure about ourselves and we can feel sure about God. Also we have the testimony of others: Godly people believe in God. There are people in the world who are atheists, but there are people in the world who are godly. By comparing them the testimony of the godly seems impressive.

The Bible as a body of literature rates consideration because of what it has done in the world; it has and still does produce and inspire Christians. The Bible talks about God. It bears record that Jesus of Nazareth talked to God. For myself, as a Christian, this is the final supreme authority. If Jesus of Nazareth looked up into heaven and talked to the Father and spoke about heaven, I can believe it. The importance of this comes to us when we read, "Without faith it is impossible to please Him, for he that cometh unto God must believe that God is and that God is a rewarder of them that diligently seek Him."

2.

Bethel

Can you feel the importance of being able to think about heaven at any time and in any place?

> And he dreamed, and behold a ladder set up on the earth, and the top of it reached to heaven: and behold the angels of God ascending and descending on it (Genesis 28:12).

The story of Jacob's ladder is common to many, although its meaning can easily be overlooked. Many Bible students today will say the interest in Old Testament times was in this world. But such a comment is not as significant as it sounds. As a matter of fact man lived on earth, so that living in this world would come first. Life started here. Man learned to live here and to talk here. It would not be surprising that the revelation of God to man should begin on this earth with men. But this is not so exceptional. Doesn't every Christian start out as a human being? Did not the Son of God become incarnate to reach us as human beings? All our language is human, earthy in origin. Does this mean that all ideas expressed in our language are only human? It is true that some people say this, but when they do we frankly think that they do not understand. We say they are in error; we call them humanists, because they would say that "man is the measure of all things."

This record of Jacob's vision in Genesis 28 corrects any false impression that the Old Testament was concerned only with the matters of this world, of the earth. Here we shall see that Jacob, just as he was beginning life on his own, was given an insight into reality. Because of what was revealed in Jacob's experience when he saw the ladder between earth and heaven, this is an important classic event in human thought.

The story begins in Genesis 28:10.

> And Jacob went out from Beersheba, and went toward Haran. And he lighted upon a certain place, and tarried there all night, because the sun was set; and he took of the stones of that place, and put them for his pillows, and lay down in that place to sleep. And he dreamed, and behold a ladder set up on the earth.

We need to consider that word "ladder." Actually, that's not the Hebrew word; and I can tell you without being too insistent about it, that there probably were no ladders, such as you and I have in mind, in those days among these tent dwelling people. The actual wording in the original language means "ascending steps" and could very well be used for a stairway. You could say that he saw a stairway, "set up on the earth, and the top of it reached to heaven." This is the important aspect: one end on earth and the other end in heaven means heaven is just as real as the earth is real.

The vision showed one means of communication from earth to heaven: both real. "And behold the angels of God ascending and descending on it." These messengers of God going up and down would mean that things here on earth mattered up there in heaven, and things up there in heaven mattered down here on earth. There's a connection between the two. This is what Jacob saw. Also it is recorded that he heard the voice of God.

> And, behold, the Lord stood above it, and said, I am the Lord God of Abraham thy father, and the God of Isaac: the land whereon thou liest, to thee will I give it, and to thy seed; and thy seed shall be as the dust of the earth, and thou shalt spread abroad to the west, and to the east, and to the north, and to the south: and in thee and in thy seed shall all the families of the earth be blessed. And, behold, I am with thee, and will keep thee in all places whither thou goest, and will bring thee again into this land; for I will not leave thee, until I have done that which I have spoken to thee of (Genesis 28:13-15).

This remarkable promise was given to Jacob as a gift. He hadn't done anything for it: he hadn't earned it. There is a wonderful truth to recognize here. When you and I get the blessing from God it will be free. It will be given to us by the grace of God. Eternal life is such a gift of God, because it is given to us.

While Jacob was lying there asleep this message came to him: "I am the Lord God of Abraham thy father, and of Isaac, and I am thy God." The Lord went on to say: "This land that you're lying on, I'm going to give it to you. Your seed is going to be so numerous it will spread everywhere. I will be with you, and I will keep you, and I will bring you back here and I'll give you everything I said I would, because I'm God." As we read this we can feel the wonderful grace of God.

What Jacob heard profoundly affected him: "And Jacob awaked out of his sleep, and he said, Surely the Lord is in this place; and I knew it not." For him this was a remarkable realization. It is just as remarkable for you and me suddenly to become aware of the fact God is here where we live. God is here: right by us! This is the very place where God is! We read that Jacob was afraid. When the Bible records that he was afraid, we have here an English translation of the Hebrew word which means he was deeply stirred. Jacob was deeply moved and said, "How dreadful is this place!" Again we should note that word "dreadful" means "awesome," "tremendous," "over-powering." As we think of ourselves being in Jacob's place, we suddenly become aware that we are standing in the presence of God, that God is right there by us. It would be enough to make us catch our breath! Stop and think! "And this is none other but the house of God": right where he was standing; "and this is the gate of heaven." What would that mean?

It means I can go from earth to heaven immediately, with nothing else between.

> And Jacob rose up early in the morning, and took the stone that he had put for his pillows, and set it up for a pillar, and poured oil upon the top of it (Genesis 28:18).

This action would indicate that he wanted to make it something special. He needed a place where he was going to worship God, "and he called the name of that place Bethel." That Hebrew word "Bethel" means "the house of God;" and the name of that city was called Luz at the first. And Jacob vowed a vow saying, "If God will be with me." This *if* is not an *if* from the standpoint of uncertainty; we get the meaning when we insert the word *since*. Thus, "Since God will be with me, and will keep me in this way that I go, and will give me bread to eat, and raiment to put on, so that I come again to my father's house in peace; then shall the Lord be my God" (Genesis 28:20-21). Jacob meant he was going to worship Him. "And this stone, which I have set for a pillar, shall be God's house." Jacob would come here to worship Him. "And of all that thou shalt give me I will surely give the tenth unto thee." This indicates that in worshipping God Jacob would use some of what God had given him to serve Him.

There are a number of lessons to learn from this incident. First of all is the important truth that earth and heaven were seen at one time, within one perspective. This indicates that heaven is just as real as the earth is real. In the next place there is a means of communication between the two: there's no gap between earth and heaven. Then in the words which Jacob heard is the truth that the will of God who made the heavens and the earth is to keep and to bless His own. All that Jacob saw; and that is what you and I can see in the record. After this we see the effect of the vision upon Jacob, "then he made his vow," since this is the gate of heaven, this is the very way in which I can come into the presence of God, I worship the Lord God. I'm going to set Him up and bow down before Him and consider He's more important than anything else; and since He is going to bless me, I'll make it a point to worship Him and to serve Him. And so he made use of this expression we all know about, "of all that thou hast given me, the tenth I will surely give to thee." Jacob did not propose to give the tithe as a means of getting the blessing of God. It was because God had blessed him, because everything he had he had from God, he would serve God and the way to serve Him was to take the tenth and serve Him in that way.

In the New Testament, John 1:51, we note that our Lord Jesus is indicating that He is Jacob's ladder for us. In communication between earth and heaven, with God's messengers ascending and descending upon it, He, the Lord Jesus, is our means of coming into the very presence of God.

3.

Heaven

Have you ever wondered whether heaven is an actual, real place? The familiar words with which the Lord's prayer begins point up the reality of heaven: "Our Father which art in heaven." Then we may remember these words of Jesus of Nazareth:

> Let not your heart be troubled: ye believe in God, believe also in me. In my Father's house are many mansions: if it were not so, I would have told you. I go to prepare a place for you. And if I go and prepare a place for you, I will come again, and receive you unto myself; that where I am, there ye may be also (John 14:1-3).

There is no question that He knew that heaven is real.

The idea of "heaven" is common to human beings everywhere. The prospect of living after this life and continuing that existence under ideal conditions has appealed to the imagination of people all over the world. The Hindus speak of "Nirvana," and for them that's heaven. The Mohammedans seem to look forward to a "paradise" of pleasure. We know that the Teutonic tribes, the Germanic people of old time, held in their hearts the conception of "valhalla" which was a sort of gallery of the great heroes. The American Indians we remember spoke of "the happy hunting ground" that their warriors would be moving toward. And other similar ideas, words and terms in the languages of mankind would indicate that poets have been inspired everywhere to dream about ideal conditions in which a person could live in uninterrupted bliss.

But the Bible concept of heaven, common to all believers, is that of a blessed home, where God is Father, and all others are brethren.

This is indicated in our songs. No doubt everyone has heard such songs as "There is a happy land, far far away;" and "When we all get to heaven, what a day of rejoicing that will be." Many have enjoyed singing, "Face to face shall I behold Him," or perhaps the glory song, "When all my labors and trials are o'er, and I am safe on that beautiful shore, just to be near the dear Lord I adore, will through the ages be glory for me. Oh, that will be, glory for me"—often we have sung, "There's a land that is fairer than day, and by faith we can see it afar." Perhaps all have joined in singing: "Shall we gather at the river, where bright angel feet have trod?" In such songs Christians have indicated confidence which they have about heaven.

In the New Testament the impression is clear that heaven is real. Jesus of Nazareth spoke of heaven. He's the One who taught us to pray, "Our Fathers which art in heaven." He's the One that told us, "I go to prepare a place for you." The apostles were men who looked up into heaven and were conscious of the realities there.

Among Christians heaven is thought of as a place where God is, as well as an experience that we want all of our loved ones to share, a destiny where we hope to be.

Actually no one knows what heaven in itself will look like. It is common to speak about the "pearly gates," and about "the streets of gold." This is the description of what was seen in a vision. The "pearly gates" would indicate a very precious entrance, and the "streets of gold" would imply very precious surroundings. But we need to remember that pearls and gold belong in this world. They are used as figures of speech. They represent something wonderful and precious. Of such heaven is composed.

Sometimes persons will say they couldn't believe in hell because they cannot conceive the flames of sulphur or the smoke of hell-fire. Actually the Bible does not say there will be sulphur there, or that anyone will see black smoke there. Here again we must recognize the language of a vision. These are figures of speech. But of this we can be sure: just as the reality of heaven will be much more precious than pearls or gold, so the reality of hell will be much more awful than sulphur or any kind of fire one can imagine.

Heaven is a real place. In thinking about heaven as a place, one should remember that this does not limit heaven to time or space. Nowhere in the Bible is it revealed where heaven is; nor are you encouraged to determine where heaven is: but it is actual and real. As a matter of fact we can know it is now! God is there now; not some day He's going to be there. He is on the Throne now! The Bible tells us that Stephen saw Him there.

Heaven is also an experience. It's an experience of love and of friendship. Perhaps you can think of some time when you've been with someone whom you love, and you enjoyed his fellowship: you probably had the most precious delight you ever have had while you were in the presence of your loved ones. Now if you could think of raising that to the "nth degree," and continuing it forever, you'd have some idea of what heaven is like. Heaven is a fellowship of love and of mutual consideration for each other. There is light and there is gladness in heaven.

The same Bible that tells about heaven tells about hell. So far as hell is concerned, you begin to get a good idea of it when you remember that there will be no fellowship with God there. There will be no love there. Nor will there be any light there. It will be dark—the blackness of darkness forever! (Jude 1:13). There'll be no one there with whom anyone can have any fellowship. It will be a matter of being in isolation. It will be a time of unbearable sadness. Cain was right when he said, "My punishment is greater than I can bear," when he was turned out to be a fugitive and a wanderer on the face of the earth, alone. Solitary confinement is the worst experience a human being can have.

Imagine falling into a bottomless pit. It is awful to be in a hole. Imagine being in a hole that has no bottom—"the bottomless pit!" Or try to think about being in such a condition in which there will be no rest: "there is no rest saith my God to the wicked." To be continually restless and never to be able to rest! Always hungry and never able to be satisfied. Always thirsty and never anything to drink. What shall we think about the fire? It will not be a fire of wood or of coal or of oil or of gas: it may be a fire of the soul. No one can be sure what that would be like.

Christians have always longed for heaven as a destiny. Many times doubts have been raised in people's minds about heaven and hell, as to whether or not they're real. No doubt many popular ideas are current, but of one thing you can feel absolutely sure; when you mention heaven that's where everybody wants his loved ones to go. And if you mention hell, despite everything that's said to depreciate it and to sneer at it and to make fun of it, nobody wants his loved ones to go there.

I can remember when I was a young Christian wanting to pray for my own family. As I was thinking about the promise that I could have anything I asked for in His name, I found myself wanting them never to be sick, never to have sorrow, never to be separated, never to die. While I was wondering about this and praying about it, it came to me as though the Father Himself were telling me: "I understand what you have in mind. You want heaven for them. That's exactly what heaven will be like: no sorrow, no crying, no tears, no separation, no night there. And I've got that ready for them. Just a little while, and when they put their trust in Me, that's where they will be."

This has been the common confidence of all believing people, of people with faith in God and in the Lord Jesus Christ. It has always been their sweet expectation to go into His presence when they pass out of this world. Paul expressed it, "absent from the body, present with the Lord."

4.

The Law of God

Can you understand how it is that the faithfulness and the integrity of God is man's greatest problem? The law of God prevails everywhere and is never changed. When you speak of the law of anything, you're referring to the usual way it has of being or doing; how it operates, regularly, always, constantly. The law of God— namely, what God will do, what God will approve, what God will endorse; prevails everywhere and is never changed. In fact, it cannot be changed because it is grounded in God Himself and He is unchangeable. It is because God Himself is always just, that the law of God is just. And He is always fair. The law of God is always fair. It's for this reason that the law is so constant, so permanent. The whole universe which God created and made, is so settled, so stable in its consistent behavior, because God holds it just that way. The result is that water is water; sugar is sugar and salt is salt. These things remain in themselves, what they are, as they are. The meaning of the law is summarized in the simple words we know so well: "Whatsoever a man soweth that shall he also reap." This is basic to everything that is.

In order to have any science it is necessary to depend on the elements to be constant. To have any kind of technology, to be able to arrange with devices and machinery in order that certain desired results will happen, things must remain constant with themselves. This is why we can use medicine: drugs are constant in themselves. It is this constancy that makes intelligent engineering possible. It makes all activity, all learning possible.

Living in this world is a dangerous business. There is no guarantee that because I am alive I am going to be well. Living in this world successfully needs the blessing of God. It is quite obvious that a man needs help to live well. We need such things as food, shelter and clothing. It is true these are available in the natural world, but a man has to work to get them. Food isn't all done up for him. It isn't even cooked. It has to be gathered and processed and prepared before it is ready for cooking. It is the same with shelter. What it takes to build a house or to make a tent is out there but the man must secure it. It is the same with clothing. What it takes to make our garments is out there but it needs to be processed. The Bible tells us God put man, Adam, in the garden and told him to dress it and to keep it. This meant that man was so to arrange and handle it as to benefit himself. Thus man acts to help himself. It is just at this point that man has trouble. When man helps himself and is successful he is tempted to become proud. Soon he becomes aware of himself and begins to think he's doing the whole thing.

As soon as a man becomes aware of himself he is tempted to become selfish. In self-consciousness he develops what we call an ego. He becomes very much aware of himself. He becomes sensitive, so that anything that in any way seems to reflect against himself makes him unhappy. He becomes suspicious of anybody that might be a rival of his.

And yet so much must be given to man. It is essential that God give it. God is the Creator, the Maker, the Provider; man in himself needs help to live. All this is true! But man becomes self-conscious and soon becomes self-centered. He gets interested in himself and becomes proud and neglects to give God the glory. He takes all the credit to himself. This is one thing that God will not allow. He will not give His glory to another.

So the situation in which man finds himself is something like this: everything man has, is given to him. The raw materials out of which he makes things, the ability to make these things, the strength to do these things, are all given to man. It's true that man must work to live. But he had to have things to work with. God gave him these. Because of his ego, because of his self-esteem, in self-consciousness man developed pride and taking all the glory to himself, he was tempted to become self-sufficient.

In all that is made, there is a basic integrity; law prevails. While man must do things in order to live, it makes a difference what he does, because as he acts certain results follow. The story of creation makes this plain. The Bible tells of the career and the fall of Adam. Adam was made of the dust of the ground. He was put in the garden and was told that he was to dress it and to keep it. Everything there was for him with one exception. He was given the commandment not to use the separated portion. There was a tree whose fruit he was not to eat, but apart from that it was all for him. Adam was tempted and fell into the sin of disobedience, bringing all men into sin. At the same time and in the same story we have the promise of the grace of God. Although man fell into sin, God in His grace brought the man into His will again, providing help for this sinning man.

The story of Babel tells how men got together to try doing something for themselves in their own strength. This was the first example of community effort and is notorious because the effort proved to be so useless. The whole truth so clearly demonstrated is that the best that man can do is not acceptable to God. Now this may seem rather harsh and it may seem rather discouraging, but it is the truth. Because man is so selfish and so proud and so self-centered, he will be foolish enough to do things that are wrong and when he does, the consequences will be wrong. "Whatsoever a man soweth that shall he also reap." The truth of the matter is that the best that man does will not be good enough to meet the demands of God.

The Old Testament account enables us to see Abraham. Abraham lived in this kind of a world. In it, it was true that "whatsoever a man soweth that shall he also reap." It was also true that Almighty God gave all things, and Abraham saw this truth. He had insight into the nature of God, and Abraham put his trust in God. He received the blessing of God in response to his obedience and received the promise that all his seed would be blessed.

Later in the record is the case of Israel, when they were slaves in the land of Egypt. They were to receive blessing from God because of the Covenant with Abraham, and so God moved to bring them out of Egypt. Israel didn't do anything for that. It wasn't anything on the part of Israel that earned it. It was given to them. God sent Moses the Deliverer, and Moses brought them out of the land of Egypt across the desert up to Canaan the Promised Land, where they were to live as God's people. While they were en route to Canaan, Moses gave them the law of God, the Ten Words, with a very simple formula, "If you do what God will approve, then you will be blessed. If you do not do what God will approve, then you will be cursed." This admonition was given to Israel as a redeemed people. This was to show these people how blessing would be earned. Israel, as the story goes, tried to operate on this basis entirely; and tried to earn their blessing. They failed, just the way Adam had failed, and anyone else would fail. The gospel reveals plainly that salvation is by faith and not by works. Because "by the works of the law shall no flesh be justified."

5.

The Weakness of Man

Can you see how the human strength of any man has very little to do with his spiritual experience as a Christian? "What is man, that thou art mindful of him?" (Psalm 8:4). These words bring to our mind the weakness and the frailty of man. James in writing about this in 4:14 says, "For what is your life? It is even a vapor, that appeareth for a little time, and then vanisheth away." Paul when speaking of himself in Romans 7:18 says, "For I know that in me, (that is, in my flesh) dwelleth no good thing." The general consensus of what the Bible has to say about man as a person would be that he is weak, that he is frail and fragile.

We all know that the Bible tells us that man was made of the dust of the earth, so we can be ready to think that he would not be strong, but the limitations of man are probably more involved in his constitution. His body for example is limited in space. He can be only in one place at any one time. At no time can he see everything. He sees only about a quarter of anything at any one look. Anyone of us looking forward from where he is can see only about twenty-five percent of all that is there. If you turn your head to see something on your right you cannot see what's on your left. If you look to see what's in front of you, you cannot see what's behind you. It is obvious that in vision man is limited.

Man is also limited in time. A man can experience now, but yesterday is gone. Tomorrow isn't here yet. So that actually so far as man is concerned, his bit of living is done here and now.

Man's vitality likewise is limited to what is given to him at his birth. If he is a strong person, vitally speaking, then he is strong. If he is a weak person so far as his body constitution is concerned, then he is weak. And in addition to all that, his attention, his outlook, his consciousness is limited by his interest in himself. The way in which he feels about himself can actually influence everything he has in mind.

As a man lives he has natural interests in self-preservation. In fact, a well-known folk saying points out: "self-preservation is the first law of nature." This is not a Christian idea. "Self-denial" is the first law of the Christian. However, it is none the less true, as far as the natural man is concerned: self-preservation is the first law of nature. A study of the psychology of man has noted that safety and security come first in human priorities. And they are essential. If a person's life is threatened, nothing else matters. That would come first. Also, hunger and thirst are imperative. When a man is hungry he will have to eat; and when he is thirsty, he will have to drink. Social interests are also strong. Fellowship is necessary. Many times a person will do anything to be with his friends, where approval is sought. These are all natural interests, such as any person has.

Out of these natural interests develops the "ego," the sense of self. As I become aware of myself and become conscious of me, it isn't long until I develop a certain pride in me, and because the ego is so close in my consciousness this tends to dominate my thinking. The consciousness of God can actually be shut out of my mind because of this consciousness of my own ego. This truth can be illustrated by the fact that a person can take a dime and hold it so close to his eye that he can't see the sun.

The weakness of man is to be seen not only in his physical condition and in his life span, but also in his failure to do the will of God. In the course of these meditations we have noted that the gospel reveals there are two worlds: man is living in this world but is related to and involved in the other world. We noted that Jacob's vision in seeing a stairway between earth and heaven, brought to our minds the truth that the things of earth matter in heaven and the things of heaven matter on earth. We have also recognized the fact that God has a certain way of doing things; that the law of God prevails throughout all creation so that everything has a way of being as it is while God works things out according to His own will. God does not change, and so it is true that "whatsoever a man soweth that shall he also reap." Because of this, it is obvious that for his own sake man should do what is right and good. This is where the trouble comes in: man is too weak to do the will of God.

The world that God has made is so constituted that in it a person must give to get. If I want to get beans, I must actually plant some beans so that I can get more beans. This means simply I must take some beans I now have and put them into the ground, actually in a sense losing them. The same would be true with a bank balance. How in the world would any person get a bank balance? Any banker will tell you: make a deposit. It will be necessary to take some money you now have in hand and give it to the bank. Thus you will in a sense give it away—but that is how you accumulate a bank balance. This principle is to be seen everywhere. As far as this world is concerned, you're going to have to "put in" if you're going to "get out." This limitation can be seen even in such a simple matter as offering to give a toy to a child. If the child is playing with toys and has both hands full of toys, and you then offer him another toy, he has a problem. Both hands are full, what's he going to do? He will have to put something away to be able to receive something new.

All this brings to mind a spiritual principle that's very, very important. You yield to God in order to win His blessing. You surrender to God that you may have His help. Perhaps you have heard it put this way: "Let go and let God."

The inability to deny self is the weakness of man. When I mention the weakness of man, I am referring to the fact that he cannot yield. He cannot surrender. He cannot let go. This is exactly where man is so often deceived. He is inclined to think that if he is to get something he should grab for it. Have you ever seen a child try to get the sunlight? Have you ever thought about that? Maybe you want to try it. Put your hand out somewhere, so that a sunbeam falls into the palm of your hand. Now try to grasp it. Close your hand quickly to grasp it. What happened? All you did was to shut it out. Your very attempt to get the sunlight shut it out. This illustrates the truth about being blessed of God. What comes from God comes freely, and it comes into an open yielded heart. Because of his sin and unbelief the natural man cannot open his heart to God. Although the living Lord says, "Behold I stand at the door and knock. If any man will open, I will come in," the natural man does not accept this.

Naturally, any human being wants satisfaction. In order to get satisfaction men eat, drink and get things. But the truth is: "a man's life consisteth not in the abundance of things which he possesseth." "Man does not live by bread alone." Satisfaction needs more than food. A man wants peace, and so in his human way, he fights to destroy his enemies. Yet he fails all the time, because peace is not achieved as the result of destroying others, but in getting along with them. So again, a man wants joy, and reaches to grab everything he can reach. He schemes and connives to beat the other fellow, thinking this will give him joy. But he is mistaken. Such procedure does not give joy. Or the man may want gladness and thinks to have gladness he must strive to get ahead of others. He enters into competition and rivalry in order to be glad. In such ways it can be seen how the natural man is blind about striving for things, deceived about gaining possessions, mistaken about real values. It seems so hard for him to realize that he can never be satisfied with food. He can never have peace by destroying others. He never can have joy by just getting things. He will never be glad because he is ahead. Man is so weak in his understanding because his desires are so strong. The Christian can be humbly grateful that he has found all satisfaction, peace, joy and gladness in fellowship with Jesus Christ. "Then were the disciples glad when they saw the Lord." It is all so gloriously true in Him: "Christ in you the hope of glory."

6.

The New Covenant

Did you realize that the Gospel of Jesus Christ promises to put the desire to do the will of God into the heart of a believer? "I will put my laws into their mind, and write them in their hearts" (Hebrews 8:10). These words are found in Scripture several times. They reveal a truth that promises real blessing for the believer.

One of the most frustrating and discouraging experiences I can have is to try to do one thing when deep down inside I want to do something else.

Much of the treatment given to conduct by teachers and preachers is aimed at telling me what to do. This actually is based on a false premise. It talks to me as if I could do what I am told, even if I would, and that's not true.

When children are young, parents teach them: this is the right thing, that is the wrong thing; because the children do not know. When the children get a little older they are expected to remember this instruction and do what is right and avoid what is wrong. But this is not what happens. When they get old enough, they develop ideas of their own as to what to do. Then instruction telling them this is right and this is wrong, coming from parents or from teachers or from preachers, becomes an annoyance. They will try to get away from it as much as they can. Just now all seem to be aware of what is called rebellion. But this is not really new: it has always been the case. Any person old enough to think for himself wants to do so. Sooner or later he will. Then he makes his own declaration of independence and starts off on his own.

Actually people do not do what is right or what is good. They do what they want to do. This is what is at the bottom of all human conduct. And this is what causes the futility, the ineptness, and the uselessness of so much preaching and teaching. I hope I will not be misunderstood. I am a preacher, and I am a teacher, and I realize very well these are occupations that can easily fall into uselessness. While I was a professor at the Seminary helping to prepare young men to preach, I would often hear sermons by students in which they labored to show what ought to be done, as if they were saying something relevant. Actually that's the kind of preaching that draws unfavorable judgment from people at large. In public life to be called a preacher is seldom flattery. Usually this designates what people judge to be useless and oft-times pointless moralizing. Often this is despised as utterly inconsequential. I remember telling the student that when he is presenting his sermon to show me what is right to do, he is assuming I would do right if I knew what it was. This is a false assumption. As a human being I do not act as I do because things are right; I act as I do because that is what I want to do.

It has been ascribed to Benjamin Franklin, and he may well have said this, that telling a person to do what he doesn't want to do, is like spitting into the wind. The person doing the instructing will just have his own words flying back into his own face.

Even when I can see it would be wise for me to act in a certain way though I actually want to act differently, sooner or later I'll do as I want to do even if it were wise to do differently. Isn't this what fills me with such unhappiness and many times with chagrin, and sometimes even with discouragement? I know right well that this is the thing I ought to do, and I go right out and do the other thing. Why? Because that's what I wanted to do.

Once at the Seminary when I was talking to a class about human conduct and human affairs, I remember one student speaking up in class to ask an earnest question: "Doctor, how is it that everything I want to do is wrong?" I was able to say: "I can tell you. I can tell you very simply, but you won't like it." "Well," he said, "tell me." I said, "Because you're you. You want to do what you want to do. Not whether it's right or wrong. It's what you like. And because you happen to be sinful, because in your heart you actually are a human being and you've got sin in you, the things you want to do aren't right. That's all. It's no big secret."

It is because of this we are often discouraged about giving advice, or giving warning to anybody. It seems there's no use in telling people what to do: they will not do what we advise anyway. Of course, as long as we care about them, we feel we must do all that we can to incline them to doing right and so we try to use a scale of rewards and punishments. And my sympathies are with people who work that way with others, trying to get them to do right by pointing out that if they do right, they'll be happy, and if they do wrong they'll be unhappy. If we have children in the home we can use this method: when they do right we reward them, and when they do wrong we punish them. Thus we try to teach them what is right and wrong. But I expect all parents find out sooner or later that in spite of everything they do, those youngsters are going to grow up to do just what they want to do. This is the human way we all have. Actually there is real value in using rewards to teach what is good, and punishment to teach them what is evil. But that doesn't change the underlying basic truth of human nature: "As a man thinketh in his heart so is he." Even when you are using rewards and punishments the children are thinking: how little do I have to do to get that reward? Or, how far can I go before I'll be punished? It is well known that rewards and punishment will not change the heart and that is like saying that righteousness will not come by the law.

We can be so glad that we know the gospel reveals something better. The gospel of the Lord Jesus Christ does not show me how to row my boat so that I'll get across the lake in spite of the storm, nor how to paddle my canoe so that I'll make sure to make it, even though the current is against me. It gives me a motor that I put on the boat to push me across the lake. Again, the gospel does not show me how to climb up ten flights of stairs without getting tired. The gospel provides me with an elevator that will lift me up those ten stair flights. The gospel does not work to repair my engine: it replaces it, it puts in a new engine. This is simply to say "You must be born again."

God sent His Son into the world to redeem those that were lost. Christ Jesus, who is the Messiah of the Old Testament, came into the world to bring to pass the possibility of deliverance for mankind. The procedure is truly unique. When Christ Jesus came to do His great work He not only came to secure my pardon, but actually He came to change me, to make me different. The Son of God came into this world incarnate as Jesus of Nazareth to enter into our situation, and in the form of man to obey His Father perfectly. Then He offered Himself as a perfect sacrifice in substitution for us, for you, for me. God allowed Jesus Christ to die for my sins. I sinned. He died for my sins. Because He died for me, I am pardoned. Now I can live forever.

Then He sent His Holy Spirit into me, into my heart, where He activates in me, inside me, the will of the Lord Jesus Christ as set forth in the Scripture. The more I read the Bible, the more I study the Bible, the more I learn the Word which the Holy Spirit can use. Then what happens to me and happens in me is that out of my heart from within me, from out of my consciousness, comes the desire, the will to be well pleasing unto God. Now, as a new born child I want to do the will of God. And that is marvelous! The only illustration like this on earth is when love fills the heart. Notice a mother taking care of her child: nothing is too much for her. She'll do anything for the baby. Or take the case of a sweetheart: a girl doing something for the young man she loves; or a youth doing something for the young girl he loves. What they do may seem altogether unreasonable, but they'll do it anyway. because they love each other. It is that way with the husband who loves his wife: he will do anything for her.

This was illustrated in the life of Jesus of Nazareth. Luke tells of the woman of the street who washed Jesus' feet with her tears and dried them with her own hair. All the Gospels tell of how Mary of Bethany came with the box of precious spikenard to anoint Jesus of Nazareth before His arrest and crucifixion. This will always be the glorious possibility in the experience of a Christian.

7.

The Meaning of Grace

Do you feel you could tell anybody what the word "grace" means? "For by grace are ye saved through faith; and that not of yourselves: it is the gift of God" (Ephesians 2:8). I grew to maturity as an unbeliever, and as I was becoming a Christian, I had everything to learn about what it meant to become a believer in Jesus Christ. My first real difficulty was to accept the idea that salvation was free. That was hard for me to believe. I didn't know of any worthwhile thing on earth that was free.

An old farmer postmaster was presenting the gospel to me. He told me salvation was "free." I remember telling the old farmer that what he was presenting to me was immoral. I said, "You're telling me I'm going to get something for nothing." I remember telling him that the only people I knew that would try to get something for nothing were thieves and crooks. And then this kind man said to me very simply, "Well, I'm expecting you to stay to have dinner with us tonight. It will be our pleasure to have you, but I don't want it to make you feel like a thief or a crook. It is true that you didn't do anything for it, but I don't want to make any profit on you. I think that perhaps about eighteen cents would cover it." He went on in a casual but unsmiling way. "What do you do at Christmastime? You can't tell everybody how you feel. When they send you anything that you haven't paid for, what do you do about it? Do you send the same thing back to them? You can't send more. If you send more back to them, you'll make thieves and crooks out of them." While I was still trying to figure out what he meant, he said to me, "How do you do at birthday time? But I suppose you've gotten all your family instructed about that." He said, "They wouldn't think of sending you anything at the time of your birthday." This was how the first glimpse of spiritual truth came into my heart and mind. You can receive something valuable from somebody else without paying anything for it if that other person wants to give it to you.

That country postmaster went on to point out to me that the finest things we know in life, between friends and in our homes, occur when one person is doing for another person without being paid for it. He kept on discussing this truth until he brought to me the idea that God was gracious, and was ready to give me salvation freely. I tried to understand it and I felt it was marvelous but it all seemed too good to be true. As he emphasized that God was no respecter of persons, that God would help anybody, I remember I exclaimed in astonishment: "Then anybody could be saved!" He smiled and assured me, "That's true." But I couldn't accept it: I felt that was too good to be true. Then he challenged me with the idea of how great God is. If He is almighty, all wise, eternal, infinite, how good could He be? If He wanted to do it, "nothing is impossible with God."

One evening he startled me by asking, "Do you know what grace means?" At that time I was a school teacher, I started to answer but I was baffled. I knew the kind of grace a woman has when she walks across the floor, but I knew that is not what is meant when the Bible says "by grace are ye saved." I knew what it was to ask grace at the table, but I was quite sure that was not what was meant by that statement: "by grace are ye saved." I was embarrassed. About that time the old man gently said to me, "Don't let it embarrass you, very few people know what it means. One reason people don't know is there is so little of it." About the only way it is commonly used is as an adjective. We may speak of a certain person being gracious, saying, "She dealt with us in a gracious manner." The idea is actually a bit like this: suppose a transient came by your house saying he was hungry. Let us say you do not want to turn away a hungry man, so you make him a sandwich and you give it to him. But really and truly he interrupted your work, so that you wished he hadn't come. You gave him the sandwich, but you would rather he had asked someone else. Now suppose that on that same day, a distinguished person came to your house about mealtime, and you invited that person to stay for a meal. Would you be wishing he wouldn't stay? No! You want him to stay and eat at your table. Actually, the meal for your distinguished friend would cost much more than the meal that you gave to that stranger. In both cases you gave the food, but in the second case, you gave the food to this distinguished friend gladly, with grace in your heart.

The old farmer helped me to see that when the Bible says "God is a God of grace," and "by grace are ye saved," God wants me to come, to believe. He wants me to receive His help and His mercy. As a matter of fact, God had reason to be offended by my conduct. As a human being I disobeyed His law, failed to thank and to honor Him. I've taken everything He's given to me and acted as if it were my own. I've ignored Him, disregarded Him; He's given me all that I have, even the very strength by which I live, but I have not thanked Him. Yet, "God commendeth his love toward us, in that while we were yet sinners, Christ died for the ungodly." What then is the grace of God? This word "grace" actually means *the undeserved kindness and favor of God toward man.*

Many years ago I had a friend who was a missionary in the African Congo. He told me of an experience that he had when he was translating a part of the New Testament into the African dialect of that particular tribe. As he was translating the Scripture, he found no word for "grace." He had difficulty in finding some way of putting into their language the meaning of the word "grace." One day he happened to be in the Chief's tent, talking to him. A maid came in and accidentally stepped on the leopard's skin that the Chief had for his own. In the customs of that tribe the leopard skin is a royal possession. No other member of the tribe is free even to touch it, let alone step on it. That was tabu. The girl having accidentally stepped on the leopard skin was liable for a grievous penalty. But the African tribal king, picking up his scepter, held it out to the girl. When she touched it, the king said a word. The girl immediately was relieved of her fears and went on about her duties. She had been pardoned. My missionary friend was greatly excited, and asked the

Chief, "What was that you said to her?" He repeated it, and the missionary said, "That's the word I want, because that's what God does with us." The Chief then told him, "The reason you haven't heard it is that only the king can use that word, it means the king pardons you." And so my friend found the word that was used for "grace" in that dialect: "grace" means "the King pardons you."

This incident can help us with the meaning of grace. When we try to understand the gospel, to realize what God has done on our behalf, we need to keep in mind that Almighty God has reached out to us and spoken the word of pardon, the word of forgiveness. We didn't deserve it. We didn't do anything for it. But out of His own inward being, out of His own grace and mercy, He reached out to us and gave to us what we couldn't earn, "the undeserved kindness and favor of God toward man." "By grace are ye saved through faith; and that not of yourselves: it is the gift of God."

8.

The Grace of God

Do you realize that it is the grace of God that causes Him to be kind and merciful?

> For ye know the grace of our Lord Jesus Christ, that, though he was rich, yet for your sakes he became poor, that ye through his poverty might be rich (II Corinthians 8:9).

This statement of the Apostle Paul brings to our minds the wonderful grace of our loving Lord. In telling the gospel to all men, we find it most difficult to get people to believe that God can be Holy and also kind. So often it is true among human beings that those who are good are often inclined to be harsh. We've seen people who in themselves seem to be good, but seldom do they seem to be kind. This may have a natural cause. I suppose that if anybody can achieve any measure of virtue it usually would be with much effort. Such people are often critical and harsh toward others who do not try as hard as they do to be good. But in the case of a Christian this would not be true; for him this principle would prevail, "freely you have received, freely give."

God gives freely. I mean "without money and without price" He will give what I need, if I but receive it. This is what we mean by "the grace of God." This is not something given occasionally, once in awhile, under some special certain condition, but in everything at any time, all the time. God is always willing and ready and rich in His grace toward all men.

Since God's help is free, you and I need to be careful to remember this means *it is not earned*. It will be given as a gift. But we must also remember God is not mocked. While God gives His grace freely, it is never cheap. We read, "Noah found grace in the eyes of the Lord." That's wonderful! But we need to keep in mind that the record also says, "Noah walked with God." Noah was spared during the flood that came upon the world destroying all men. He was delivered from that judgment, but he had to come into the ark. He wasn't given a special place here on earth where the water wouldn't reach him. The way he was delivered was by his getting into the ark. This same truth was seen in the case of Abraham. Abraham is called "the friend of God." The Bible records that he received the promise of God's blessing. But what does the Bible say about him? "Abraham obeyed God, and he went out not knowing whither he went." He did what God wanted him to do, and so received the blessing of God.

We note that Paul urged believers: "We then beseech you also that ye receive not the grace of God in vain" (II Corinthians 6:1). Apparently receiving the grace of God should not be a careless matter. Consider again the case of Noah. All the world was sinful so that the thoughts of men's hearts everywhere were only evil. They were all to be destroyed. Noah, among all the doomed people, received the grace of God and he was spared. Marvelously wonderfully true! But, he had to act, he had to get into the ark and stay there. His getting into the ark separated him from the other people. This was the condition under which he was spared. Now look again at the case of Abraham. Of all the people in his day and time, he was the one who received the promise of God. Abraham heard God say, "Get thee out of thy country, out of thy father's house, out from thy kindred, into a land that I will show thee." He had to leave! He had to be separated from, in order that he might enter into, the situation in which God would be with him.

This truth can be seen also in the case of Israel, the Nation of God, the People of God. To receive the blessing and the grace of God they had to get out of Egypt. They had been there over four hundred years, but now they were to come out of it. What we are noting is that receiving the grace of God, so free and so wonderful, requires and is contingent upon obeying God. By coming out of where you've been and coming into where God wants you, you will receive the blessing. This will not be as a reward, nor because you earned it. It will come to you as a gift, but only when you are obedient to God.

When Paul urged the Corinthians not to receive the grace of God in vain, he gave them instructions:

> Be ye not unequally yoked together with unbelievers: for what fellowship hath righteousness with unrighteousness? and what communion hath light with darkness? And what concord hath Christ with Belial? or what part hath he that believeth with an infidel? And what agreement hath the temple of God with idols? for ye are the temple of the living God; as God hath said, I will dwell in them, and walk in them; and I will be their God, and they shall be my people. Wherefore come out from among them, and be ye separate, saith the Lord, and touch not the unclean thing; and I will receive you, and will be a Father unto you, and ye shall be my sons and daughters, saith the Lord Almighty. Having therefore these promises, dearly beloved, let us cleanse ourselves from all filthiness of the flesh and spirit, perfecting holiness in the fear of God (II Corinthians 6:14–7:1).

The blessing of God is free! Certainly, the grace of God is wonderful and rich, and it will be given to those who belong to Him.

Consider the instance of the bride! She shares all that belongs to the bridegroom. But it needs to be noted: she now belongs to him only. She shares everything with him because she is his. Eternal life is to be received as a gift. Thank the Lord! But only by those who belong to the Lord.

There are two aspects in the grace of God. Come and receive. Buy without money and without price, what God has for you. Absolutely! It's given to you freely. The other aspect is, be totally committed unto Him: altogether His.

"And God is able to make all grace abound toward you; that ye, always having all sufficiency in all things, may abound in every good work" (II Corinthians 9:8). This is wonderfully true for you! God will give you an inward strength that will enable you to meet every situation and respond to His will at all times. That strength, that blessing, that grace of God which comes from God, is freely given. We can say we are "being justified freely by His grace through the redemption that is in Christ Jesus." This we cannot achieve in our own strength. For this we need the help of God.

Paul was reminded of this when he had his thorn in the flesh and asked God again and again to take it away: it was shown to him that God wanted it to be there. Paul might very easily have felt in his heart: "I can't stand it. I can't bear it." But this is what God said to him. "My grace is sufficient for thee." No matter what your situation may be, remember that the things that are happening to you are under God. He is watching over you, and His grace will be sufficient for you. He'll give it to you, it will be adequate. But you must belong to Him. Turn yourself over to Him. Commit yourself entirely to Him. Then He will bless you with Himself, for His Name's sake.

9.

The Gospel of Christ

Do you understand why the gospel of Jesus Christ is called Good News? "According to the glorious gospel of the blessed God." Apparently in the New Testament every reference to what God is going to do in the name of Jesus Christ indicates it will be wonderful, and glorious. But is this what people commonly think?

When a person speaks of the gospel, he is generally referring to preaching. We call any man who is a preacher a minister of the gospel. When a man is presenting a message we ask, "What kind of gospel is he preaching?" Do we realize the word "gospel" should also mean good news, glad tidings?

When I was a boy, I went to church regularly. But for some reason it was never a glad time. I cannot remember I ever saw anyone who was glad to go into church. I can remember the men standing around outside the church, waiting for the last minute before they'd go in. They didn't seem glad. It seemed this was a duty that they would perform. My impression was that the only glad thing about a church service was the pronouncing of the benediction. It always seemed to me when folks were getting ready to leave that's when they began to feel good. Of course, I was just a boy, but was I wrong?

I am afraid things were much the same with me. I must confess that when I thought of praying I thought of something long and tedious. When I thought about preaching, I thought of something tiresome. I always wished the preacher would finish. I was often afraid he wouldn't ever finish, that he'd just keep on, keep on, keep on, and I was just tired of the whole business. As for the midweek prayer service, we didn't have one. We lived in the country. Afterwards when I lived in town where there were more people I found there were other church services. The impression I got was that even for the people who did go to the evening service, midweek prayer service, Wednesday night service or Thursday night service, it always seemed like an extra chore: the kind of thing you'd get out of if you could.

Consider what has happened to the Sunday evening service. There was a time when nearly all churches had morning and evening services, but now it seems to me that the wish of the majority has finally prevailed: feeling that the Sunday evening service was unnecessary many churches just stopped it. Would any one say the message preached in such churches was one of good news? That would have been a surprise to me! Glad tidings? Not the ones I heard. But is this the way it should be?

What does the Bible say? Actually the word "evangel" means the good news. In what sense is the Bible message good? The Bible tells us how "the Son of man is come to seek and to save that which was lost." There are three great stories in Luke 15 which tell of joy. First, is the story of the lost sheep. The shepherd noticed one sheep was missing. He went out to find it. He left the ninety-nine safe in the fold and went out to search for the lost sheep until he found it. When he found that sheep, he put it on his own shoulders and brought it home, saying, "Rejoice with me. I have found my sheep." The Lord Jesus tells us, "There is joy in the presence of the angels of God over one sinner that repenteth."

In that same chapter is the story of the lost coin. The woman had ten coins. She missed one, nine were safe. She put the nine safe ones away, took her broom and swept diligently seeking the coin that was lost. When she found it, she called in her neighbors, saying, "Rejoice with me. Be glad with me. I've found the coin that was lost."

The third story in that chapter is the wonderful story of the Prodigal Son. It was very natural that the young man wanted to be away from home. The sad story of how he lost everything that he had is not really surprising. The important thing was the way in which he made up his mind to go home: "I will go home. I will say to my father, I have sinned and I am not worthy to be called thy son. Make me as one of thy hired servants." On his way home, his father saw him coming a long way off and ran out to meet him. His very return spoke of the change in his heart. When the father recognized this, he exclaimed, "Bring hither the fatted calf, bring hither the best robe and put it on him and put rings on his fingers and shoes on his feet, we are going to rejoice. This my son was dead, and is alive again."

The older brother couldn't understand the rejoicing but the father didn't rebuke him. He didn't scold him. He went out and reasoned with him. He told the older brother, "Listen, your brother was dead. He's changed. He's different. He's alive again." And then he makes this statement, "It was meet (it was proper) that we should make merry, and be glad."

If ever you have the privilege of being in a church service where sinners are coming to God, where people are turning to God, you will recognize a church service where there is joy. There will be gladness. The singing of the hymns will be strong while the people really and truly rejoice: "At the cross, at the cross, where I first saw the light, and the burden of my sins rolled away. It was there by faith I received my sight and now I am happy all the day." You will be able to share in the joy: "There is a fountain filled with blood, fresh from Immanuel's veins. And sinners plunged beneath that flood, lose all their guilty stains." You will realize it is a joyful thing to be reconciled to God.

In a time of sickness it is wonderful to see the doctor. Have you ever had any real sickness, real suffering, pain, and you wanted someone to come and help, and you waited and waited, and then do you remember what it was like when you saw the doctor coming? Have you ever been lost, so that you didn't know your location or how to get to where you wanted to be? What a wonderful thing to see somebody that knew, or a familiar landmark. Such experiences will help us to realize what a wonderful blessing it is to come to know Christ. What we are thinking about can be seen in the Old Testament in a touching story in the life of David (II Samuel 9). As a young man David had a very wonderful friend, Jonathan, the son of Saul, the King. In a mutual agreement they promised never to forget each other. Jonathan asked David to promise him that when David became king he would remember Jonathan's family and be gracious to them. Jonathan was killed in battle. Saul lost his life, and David was put on the throne. Remembering his promise to Jonathan, David sent out the word, "Is there not one of the house of Saul to whom I can show the grace of God?" Someone came and told him, "There is one. He is Jonathan's son but he's a cripple. His name is Mephibosheth [Me-phib-o-sheth]." David said, "Bring him to me." And when that was done, David said to him, "Fear not: for I will surely show thee kindness for Jonathan thy father's sake, and will restore thee all the land of Saul thy father; and thou shalt eat at my table continually." And so it was arranged. This is a classic example of grace. This lame man who once had been a rebel, an opposing enemy, defeated in battle, with all his property confiscated, and his life in danger, was now brought into the presence of the victorious king. To his amazement he was pardoned, and his property was restored. But even more than that: a special place was made for him at the king's table! This remarkable story ends with this phrase, "And he was lame on both his feet." This always profoundly stirs me because here is exactly a picture of myself. God came for me when I wasn't worthy. He called me to Himself, and made me "an heir of God, a joint-heir with Jesus Christ." And not only that, but He actually has arranged that I should never be alone. I should always have a place at the King's table. And all that was done for me in spite of the fact that in my own weakness and sinfulness, I was lame on both my feet.

10.

Man Is Lost

Did you know that the Bible teaches that all human beings are lost and need to be saved? "For the Son of man is come to seek and to save that which was lost" (Luke 19:10). What a marvelous truth these words convey and how my heart is called to them again and again! People differ, but there is one way in which they are all alike. "All have sinned and come short of the glory of God." "You must be born again." This is true for everybody. "Flesh and blood cannot inherit the kingdom of God." This statement covers all human beings. No one as he is can enter into that Father-Son relationship with God that will bring him into the Kingdom of God. "You must be born again."

We are dependent on so many things in order to live; air, food, water. We did not make this world, and cannot control it. As great as medicine is, man cannot prolong his life beyond the last heartbeat. When his heart stops beating, that's the end. While it is true that man can manage a lot, and human beings are active in bringing many things to pass, in the last analysis man can do very little about the world and about life. God is the Creator, Keeper, Judge, and Savior. He alone is Almighty. If man is ever going to have any real help for living it must come from God. The marvelous truth is God is prepared and wants to give it. The Bible says, "For the eyes of the Lord run to and fro throughout the whole earth, to show himself strong in the behalf of them whose heart is perfect toward him" (II Chronicles 16:9). Because of sin, man's own personal wrong-doing, man is out of touch with God. Man is lost, condemned for sin. "The soul that sinneth it shall die." Ezekiel 18:20. So for the natural man there is nothing to look forward to but death. Many feel this to be true: "all their lifetime subject to bondage." Their prospect is darkness. Such a person feels alone and in the dark. All that he holds

47

dear and cherishes, he may lose. The natural man faces death and destruction. Isaiah felt this when he said, "Woe is me! for I am undone; because I am a man of unclean lips, and I dwell in the midst of a people of unclean lips." Man's very nature is selfish and proud.

Man is also sensitive about anything that affects him. Paul wrote, "I know that in me, that is in my flesh, there dwelleth no good thing." You'll find this not only in the Bible, but in your own personal experience. The natural man, just as he is, on his own without God, is without hope in the world. When God calls and man fails to respond he is on his own, alone, lost! Dear reader, if by some chance this should be your case, where are you going? That's the question that God asked Adam when He said, "Adam, where art thou?" Remember the three parables in Luke 15 about the lost? First the parable of the lost sheep. The shepherd had one hundred sheep and ninety-nine were safe at home. One had wandered away and was lost. The shepherd went to seek it. Then the parable of the woman with the ten coins. She lost a coin and hunted diligently for it. Then the parable of the Prodigal. The father had two sons, and one went away.

These parables are different from each other to some extent. The lost sheep knew it was lost, but it didn't know the way home. That seems to be a clear picture of many who are lost. The lost coin didn't even know it was lost, but it was lost nonetheless. The lost son knew he was lost. He knew he was away from his father and he knew the way home. They were alike in this: all were lost. And they were all alike in the final result: all were found, the good shepherd went out seeking that lost sheep. The careful woman took the broom and swept her house diligently, seeking that lost coin. And the faithful father was waiting for that wandering son, that lost son. The greatest thing you can say to the soul that is lost is "God so loved the world, that he gave his only begotten Son, that whosoever believeth in him should not perish, but have everlasting life." Look up where you are and come to God: God is looking for you. He will reach down and find you for Himself.

11.

Christ Has Come

Do you realize that Jesus Christ makes all the difference between people? "The Master is come and calleth for thee." These are the words that Martha took to Mary her sister, on that day when Jesus of Nazareth came to visit them after their brother Lazarus had died. They had sent for Him. Days had gone by and He had not come. Now finally, He came. First Martha met Him and talked with Him. Then she ran in to tell Mary, saying, "The Master is come, and calleth for thee" (John 11:28). This is the word that we would like to take to believers everywhere: God has sent His Son into the world.

The name of Jesus Christ is widely known and yet it is possible that few actually understand Him. To be blessed of God, I need to believe in Him. To believe in Him, I need to understand Him. There is a popular notion that Christ brings people together. This can be a most misleading idea. Jesus of Nazareth said:

> Whosoever therefore shall confess me before men, him will I confess also before my Father which is in heaven. But whosoever shall deny me before men, him will I also deny before my Father which is in heaven. Think not that I am come to send peace on earth: I came not to send peace, but a sword. For I am come to set a man at variance against his father, and the daughter against her mother, and the daughter-in-law against her mother-in-law. And a man's foes shall be they of his own household. He that loveth father or mother more than me is not worthy of me: and he that loveth son or daughter more than me is not worthy of me. And he that taketh not his cross, and followeth after me, is not worthy of me. He that findeth his life shall lose it: and he that loseth his life for my sake shall

find it. He that receiveth you receiveth me, and he that receiveth me receiveth him that sent me. He that receiveth a prophet in the name of a prophet shall receive a prophet's reward; and he that receiveth a righteous man in the name of a righteous man shall receive a righteous man's reward. And whosoever shall give to drink unto one of these little ones a cup of cold water only in the name of a disciple, verily I say unto you, he shall in no wise lose his reward (Matthew 10:32-42).

Christ Jesus did not come to bring men together, He came to bring men to God.

It is true that some will respond and will be saved. But some will not respond, and will not be saved. Jesus of Nazareth is not some sort of an elective possibility, making it possible to become spiritual if one should want to do so. This is not an adequate way to look at Him. Jesus of Nazareth was the Son of God and He came for all men. They all need Him and He will save "whosoever believeth in him." He is no respecter of persons. It matters for eternity what any man will do with Him.

In the beginning was the Word, and the Word was with God, and the Word was God. The same was in the beginning with God. All things were made by him; and without him was not any thing made that was made. In him was life; and the life was the light of men. And the light shineth in darkness; and the darkness comprehended it not . . .That was the true Light, which lighteth every man that cometh into the world. He was in the world, and the world was made by him, and the world knew him not. He came unto his own, and his own received him not . . . And the Word was made flesh, and dwelt among us, (and we beheld his glory, the glory as of the only begotten of the Father,) full of grace and truth (John 1:1-5, 9-11, 14).

It is most important that each soul should recognize that Jesus of Nazareth actually was and now is the Son of God. When Jesus of Nazareth asked Peter: "And whom do you say that I am." Peter was able to testify: "Thou art the Christ the Son of the living God." It is true that when the Son of God became incarnate as Jesus of Nazareth He was humble, meek, and lowly in heart. He came as a servant, but *He was the Lord.* Christians today must beware they do not adopt popular ideas about Jesus Christ. We must remember that when we see Him in pictures, we are looking at what the artist thinks. When we read about Him in theology, we are reading what some scholar thinks. We cannot see the truth about Him in songs that people sing, nor in verses the poets write. He Himself told us how to find out about Himself: "Search the scriptures, for they are they that testify of me."

So we turn to the Bible to learn the answer to "What think ye of Christ?" In Scripture we read He is "the One, of whom Moses and the prophets did write." Paul wrote a wonderful description of Him:

> In whom we have redemption through his blood, even the forgiveness of sins: who is the image of the invisible God, the first-born of every creature: for by him were all things created, that are in heaven, and that are in earth, visible and invisible, whether they be thrones, or dominions, or principalities, or powers: all things were created by him, and for him: and he is before all things, and by him all things consist. And he is the head of the body, the church: who is the beginning, the first-born from the dead; that in all things he might have the pre-eminence (Colossians 1:14-18).

The name of Jesus Christ stands out in all the world as supreme in history. About Jesus Christ, you could say He's like the sun in the heavens. Men didn't put Him up there and men can't take Him down. The Scriptures show Him to be unchangeable. Humble as He was, Jesus Christ never apologized to anybody. He made concessions to no man. He was at all times the Lord. He stands as a great Rock in the river of human history: "He that hath the Son hath life; and he that hath not the Son of God hath not life." No wonder Pilate, when faced with this Person, Jesus of Nazareth, exclaimed, "What shall I do then with Jesus that is called Christ?"

12.

Whosoever Will May

Have you ever wondered just how much truth is in the idea that one man is as good as another?

And the Spirit and the bride say, Come. And let him that heareth say, Come. And let him that is athirst come. And whosoever will, let him take the water of life freely (Revelation 22:17).

One of the outstanding aspects of the gospel which we rejoice to hear is that God is no respecter of persons. "Whosoever will may come." "If any man will do his will, he shall know of the doctrine." It has been well said that at the foot of the cross the ground is level. Everybody is on the same basis. I've often appreciated the Bethlehem story of the birth of Jesus of Nazareth with the babe lying in the manger. I grew up on the farm, and this enabled me to understand something very well: anyone can come to Him. Of course, the rich can come if they would, and the strong and the famous are welcome. But poor people, weak people, people who never amount to a great deal in public, who live quiet, obscure lives who might shrink from coming if He were in a palace, can come so easily because He was lying in a stable! In a manger! Surely anybody can come.

And it is just that simple to become a Christian. Anyone who can die, can become a Christian. Dying is very simple. You can do it when you're so weak you can't do anything else. Dying is easy, but it's very profound. And so it is with the matter of coming to the Lord. It's not in what you know that makes you a Christian, so you do not have to try to learn everything. Nor is it in what you can do, since you cannot be trained to enable you to become a believer. It is not even in what you have done: any sort of review of your good record. You don't have to be rich, but you don't have to be poor. You don't have to be educated, but you don't have to be ignorant either. You don't have to be good. (I'm so glad!) But you don't have to be bad. Anybody can come as he is.

At this point we must take care to avoid a common error. It is sometimes said that it is a wholly Christian idea that one person is as good as another. That is not true! You might as well say that one person is just as tall as another. You know better! There is a profound and wonderful truth in this that any person has just as much privilege to come into the presence of God as anybody else. In this sense there is an equality. Any person can come—every person can come, regardless of who he is or what he is. This is not because he is the same as everybody else, but because Christ Jesus died for him as well as for others.

This truth has been a great comfort to many. Some souls have trouble. They don't seem to get an even start with other people. They may have been blemished. They may have had things to overcome. All such persons can be assured there is no barrier to hinder them from turning to God. It is also wonderful to be able to remember when we are tempted to ask God, "Why has thou made me thus?" that it doesn't really make any difference. You're not big? You're not small? You're not strong? You're not weak? You're not rich? You're not poor? None of that matters; "Whosoever will may come."

This does not mean everyone will come. It's a grievous error to say all will be saved, none will be lost. That's not true! Turn to the Scriptures. Jesus of Nazareth taught:

> Enter ye in at the strait gate: for wide is the gate, and broad is the way, that leadeth to destruction, and many there be which go in thereat: because strait is the gate, and narrow is the way, which leadeth unto life, and few there be that find it (Matthew 7:13-14).

He gave further warning:

Not every one that saith unto me, Lord, Lord, shall enter into the kingdom of heaven; but he that doeth the will of my Father which is in heaven. Many will say to me in that day, Lord, Lord, have we not prophesied in thy name? and in thy name have cast out devils? and in thy name done many wonderful works? And then will I profess unto them, I never knew you: depart from me, ye that work iniquity (Matthew 7:21-23).

The well-known parable of the wise and foolish virgins (Matthew 25:1-13) teaches this same truth. Five were wise and five were foolish. They that were foolish took their lamps and took no oil with them, but the wise took oil in their vessels with their lamps. While the bridegroom tarried, they all slumbered and slept. At midnight there was a cry, "Behold the bridegroom cometh. Go out to meet Him." Then all those virgins arose and trimmed their lamps. The foolish said unto the wise, "Give us of your oil, for our lamps are gone out." But the wise answered saying, "Not so, lest there be not enough for us and you. Go rather to them that sell and buy for yourselves." And while they went to buy, the bridegroom came and they that were ready went in with them to the marriage and the door was shut. Afterward came also the other virgins saying, "Lord, Lord, open to us." But He answered and said, "Verily, I say unto you, I know you not. Watch therefore for you know neither the day nor the hour when the Son of Man cometh."

There is no possible way to misunderstand what the Lord is saying here. Anyone can come to God but not everyone will. Since human nature is as weak as it is, it's always a dangerous thing to be rich. The rich man might not come. If a man is strong, he might not feel the need. If a man is clever, he might be tempted to depend on his own wits. The person who is young might think he has a long time coming. Or if a woman is beautiful, she might be fooled by the way people look at her that she does not need any help. Yet it is wonderfully true that even if you were any one or all those things, you could still come to God. A person can be rich or poor, strong or

weak, smart or dull, young or old, beautiful or plain: all are welcome. "Whosoever will, may come" and can be saved, and will be
saved. Then "let us come boldly to the throne of grace, that we may
find grace to help in the time of need."

13.

The New Birth

Do you understand why the Bible teaches that in order to have the blessing of God a man must be born again? In speaking to Nicodemus as reported in John 3:5 Jesus of Nazareth made a clear straightforward statement that doesn't allow any kind of misunderstanding: "Verily, verily, I say unto thee, Except a man be born of water and of the Spirit, he cannot enter into the kingdom of God."

This new birth is not a rebirth. It's not starting over again. It is another birth, a different one. Any intelligent, sincere person has in his heart the great desire: he feels the need to have the blessing of God. To have the blessing of God obedience is essential! If I want God to bless me, I must do His will. It's "they that do the will of God that shall abide forever."

What would be involved in obeying God? First, I must reverence God. The person who is obeying Him and living a life of obedience will honor God. He will remember that God made him, that God keeps him, that God overrules in watching over him, that God guides him, and that God strengthens him. Everything he has comes from God. "Every good and perfect gift cometh from above" and that will cause the man in himself to want to thank God and praise God.

Then I must respect those that are in authority over me. In life as you and I live it, there are some people who have responsibility about us, over us, to direct us, to guide us, to protect us or to take care of us. I must respect such and honor such. I must respect those that are in authority.

I must be considerate of my equals, others round about me. Finally, there will be some people not as well off as I am, nor as strong. In all kindness I would recognize them as the poor and needy. To such I must exercise charity. In all of this or any part of it, I must deny myself. The practical problem in all this is manifested in Scripture at the very beginning of the life of man. Adam was put in the garden and given everything in there for his own use. He was told of one tree there of which he was not to eat. It was put within his reach as a separated portion, and he was given the commandment not to eat of it. This required Adam to control himself: to put himself under discipline about this matter in order that he might obey God. This is God's way of dealing with man. It is true to this day, so far as living is concerned, that if I want the blessing of God I must obey Him. Obeying God will always mean I must deny myself. I cannot do as I will.

Such self-denial is impossible for sinful man. This is what Nicodemus had in mind when he came to the Lord. He had heard the Lord speak, and he had seen Him work. He came to Him privately to ask Him, "How in the world can this be done? How can it be done, human nature being what it is? Self-preservation being the first law of nature, how can anybody undertake to live this way in which you deny yourself all the way through?" The Lord answered him, "You must be born again. You're going to have to work on another basis than that which you're working on now. Being the kind of person you are now, you can never do it, but you can be a different kind of person when you would be born again of the Spirit of God."

This new birth is not a rerun, a chance to do it all over again so that you can try to avoid the mistakes. It is actually a different kind of life which enables one to have a different way of doing things. Jesus of Nazareth said, "If any man will be my disciple, let him deny himself." That's the way it still must be. As a child of Adam, as a human being, in my own ego I could hear that, and I could try to do it. I could try to deny myself, but I would fail because of the sin that is in me. The sin in me causes me to be selfish and no matter how I would try to deny myself I would twist things around, so that in my very performance of what I thought was God's will for me I would be trying to advance myself in some fashion. But as a child of

God, born again, Christ Jesus would do it in me. He said of Himself, "I do always the things that please my Father." Paul could say about himself, "I am crucified with Christ; nevertheless I live; yet not I, but Christ liveth in me." This was the basis of the confidence Paul had as he lived.

When Jesus of Nazareth taught "The Son of man must be lifted up," He was referring to the fact that He Himself must be put to death. At Calvary the flesh, godly flesh, holy flesh, sinless flesh, but nonetheless flesh, was crucified. If I want to walk in the Lord that I may be blessed in this fashion, I must be crucified: I must deny myself and yield to the Lord. This must go on and on as long as I live in this body on this earth.

"He must increase but I must decrease." Growth is possible. When we are born in Christ and become babes in Him, we can grow. This growing in Christ Jesus has been indicated in a poem that is also used as a hymn. As I remember the first verse describes a certain spiritual condition which the poet regretted, when in his heart it was "all of self, none of Thee." The next verse refers to certain changes that took place in the man's life, so that he could say, "Some of self, and some of Thee." But as time went on and God had worked in his heart by His grace and led him through various experiences, he was able to report with satisfaction, "Less of self and more of Thee." And then in the closing verses, he gives expression to his prayer, a longing prayer that the time would come when it would be true that he could say, "None of self and all of Thee."

All that I have discussed is involved in the new birth. I put my trust in the Lord, yielding myself to Him. I find that I am being put to death as I let Him have His way in me. By His grace I am enabled to put Him first in my own heart and thus I grow more and more.

To understand the new birth more fully I should be using such words as natural, born again, carnal, spiritual, and filled with the Spirit. Natural will indicate the way I was when I was born of my human parents. Born again will refer to the new birth, when I have a new life starting in me by the grace of God. Carnal will mean my state when the new life in me is real, but the old life still dominates. Spiritual will refer to the state when the new life gains control, and the "old man" in me is put under control. The "old man" is still there, but as I commit myself to walk in the ways of the Lord I am now spiritual. As a spiritually minded person I can look forward to something I would hope for and pray to God would happen again and again, namely: to be filled with the Spirit. In this state everything in my consciousness would be yielded to the Lord Jesus Christ Himself.

14.

Babes in Christ

Can you understand that when a person accepts Christ, and becomes a Christian, he does not know everything all at once?

"As newborn babes, desire the sincere milk of the word, that ye may grow thereby" (I Peter 2:2). New Christians are to count themselves as newborn babes and then to desire the sincere milk of the Word that they may grow thereby. Peter is instructing Christians to read and study the Bible; to get to know the Bible that they might grow as Christians. When a person first accepts Christ Jesus as Savior and Lord, he belongs to the Lord. He has been received into the family of God. Naturally he is just a beginner; having accepted Christ he has everything to learn about living with Him.

When a young couple give themselves to each other in a wedding ceremony there will be many things for them that are new, and much to learn. And that's the way it is with a Christian. I accept Christ Jesus as my Savior and Lord on the simple basis that I know I am a sinner, I deserve to be condemned, but I believe He has come to bring me to God. I believe that God will for Christ's sake forgive me. I want forgiveness. I accept Christ. Now I have forgiveness. But that is just a beginning. Now I am a babe in Christ. I must now learn what that means as I live.

The one thing that babies can do, even though they're just babies, is grow. For that they will need food. The New Testament indicates that there is a special food that should be kept for young Christians. You'll find this in the book of Hebrews 5:12—6:2:

> For when for the time ye ought to be teachers, ye have need that one teach you again which be the first principles of the

oracles of God [and that phrase "the first principles" means the abc's], and are become such as have need of milk, and not of strong meat. For every one that useth milk is unskillful in the word of righteousness: for he is a babe. But strong meat belongeth to them that are of full age, even those who by reason of use have their senses exercised to discern both good and evil. Therefore leaving the principles [the abc's] of the doctrine of Christ, let us go on unto perfection; not laying again the foundation of repentance from dead works, and of faith toward God, of the doctrine of baptisms, and of the laying on of hands, and of resurrection of the dead, and of eternal judgment.

Those are the first things that a Christian learns, the abc's. In turning to God, I must repent; I must admit myself to be unfit, that the things I've done are not right in the sight of God. Then I must have faith toward God. I put my trust in God.

I know that I can use the word "faith" when referring to a chair that I sit on, to a car that I drive, to medicine that I take but now I use it about God. I hear that Christ Jesus died for me. I understand that salvation is open and free for me. I know that God has offered to save me. Now I believe in Him.

Next, I learn about baptisms, washing, cleansing. After I become a Christian, there are a great many things in my life that may need to be washed away. The "laying on of hands" may mean I receive a sense of commission, accepting responsibility. When I become a Christian and Christ is now "in me" I will have things to do. "The resurrection of the dead" can mean that when I believe in the Lord Jesus Christ I have the privilege of living in "newness of life." I don't have to live in "the old man." I can actually be in "the new man." These are the things that are basic.

As the Christian grows he will practice repentance. Not just once and for all, but again and again as long as he lives. What does it mean when I repent? Repentance is not a matter of being sorry for the wrong I have done. The wrong I have done may be something I should be sorry for, but that is not repentance. Nor is it promising to do better. To promise improvement may be very impressive, but it doesn't mean much. If I promise you I'm going to do better tomorrow, you have the right to ask me, "Why did you do what you did yesterday?" I probably did what I did because I am as I am, and as long as I am as I am I will do it again. Promising to do better doesn't mean much! Repentance is a drastic revolutionary judgment upon myself. I recognize I'm not any good in the sight of God. Paul says, "I know that in me, that is in my flesh, there dwelleth no good thing." Job says in speaking to God: "I have heard of thee with the hearing of the ear, but now mine eye seeth Thee, and I abhor myself in dust and ashes." Moses said with reference to himself, "I can't do it. I haven't got it in me to do it. I can't speak. I can't do the thing you've asked me to do." Isaiah said about himself, "Woe is me! I am undone. I am a man of unclean lips and I dwell in the midst of a people of unclean lips." These are all examples of repentance, and this is a normal healthy exercise of any person coming to God.

With reference to self, I repent; but with reference to Christ, I believe. With reference to self, the repentant soul denies the self; with reference to God, because of the faith I have in Him I receive Christ Jesus. With reference to me, I surrender myself. With reference to Christ Jesus, I walk in Him. With reference to self: I yield myself under the mighty hand of God; with reference to Christ Jesus I live in Him. This shows "if any man be in Christ, he is a new creature." The problem of the babe in Christ, the beginner, is really simple. My natural self, my own ego, promises me satisfaction and honor, but it's not true. I won't get it. My spiritual being with "Christ in you the hope of glory" leads me in the will of God into conflict with myself in inner opposition against the flesh, but with satisfaction and victory.

So as a babe in Christ I face a very simple issue: will I serve self or will I serve Christ? As I grow I will experience that "He must increase and I must decrease." As I yield to Him in repentant faith there will be less and less of me; but as I grow in grace and knowledge, there will be more and more of Him.

This promises "Glory for me!!"

15.

A New Creature

Do you realize that when a person becomes a Christian, he enters into a spiritual warfare?

> Therefore if any man be in Christ, he is a new creature: old things are passed away; behold, all things are become new (II Corinthians 5:17).

When a person becomes a Christian, he is immediately involved in a constant warfare between the flesh and the Spirit. He has in him two natures. He has in him the human nature which Paul calls the flesh. Everything he received from his parents, which is centered in his body and is in this world, is meant by "the flesh." But when he has accepted Christ Jesus, believing in the Word of God and receiving from God the grace that is in Christ Jesus, he is born again and has in him now Christ the hope of glory.

Thus the Christian has in himself two different natures, contrary to each other. Paul had this in mind when he said, "For the flesh lusteth against the Spirit, and the Spirit against the flesh: and these are contrary the one to the other: so that ye cannot do the things that ye would" (Galatians 5:17). The Christian has in him the "old man," his old human nature, which has desires that are not like God. At the same time he has in him the new nature, that which comes through Christ Jesus and which is not like his own self. Thus the Christian wants to do what appeals to his body, but he also wants to do what appeals to his soul. These are contrary, the one to the other, so that he cannot do the things that he would. And so it follows that the Christian is never really as good as he would like to be because the flesh is dragging him down; but he is never really as bad as he could be, because the Spirit is pulling him up. And so the Christian is involved in this tension between these two natures, "the flesh and the Spirit."

The Christian needs to be guided by the Word of God that would lead him into blessing. To begin with, he has a certain attitude toward himself, i.e., a matter of constantly judging himself in repentance. Paul describes this conflict in Romans 7:14-25. "For we know that the law is spiritual: but I am carnal, sold under sin. For that which I do I allow not." That is to say the very things I practice are not the things that I approve. "For what I would," what I really want to do, "that do I not." I don't practice the very things I want to do. "But what I hate [what I'm against], that do I." That's the very thing that I'm practicing. "If then I do [that is, I practice] that which I would not [what I really don't want to do] I consent unto the law that it is good." The very fact I don't want to do the wrong means that I am admitting that the law of God is right, and that I'd like to do it that way. "Now then it is no more I that do it, but sin that dwelleth in me. For I know that in me, (that is, in my flesh) dwelleth no good thing: for to will is present with me; but how to perform that which is good I find not." In this graphic way Paul describes the plight of many who believe.

We can learn from our own personal experience in living. Do you remember the last time you fell down? Did you want to? Did you just throw yourself on the ground? Well, why did you fall? You fell because the law of gravity was pulling you down. When you lost your balance, down you went. You didn't have to work at it. This is what Paul is saying. A believing person can be so attuned to the Spirit that in his heart and mind he wants to do the will of God, but in his own personality, in himself, he has the disposition to do the things that are natural and that are of the flesh, even though they are not the will of God. "For the good that I would [the very thing that I want to do that's good] I do not." I don't practice it. "But the evil which I would not [the very thing I don't want to do] that I do. Now if I do that I would not [if that's the case with me, that I'm practicing the very thing I don't want to do] it is no more I that do it, but sin that dwelleth in me." In this way Paul indicates that there is operative in him constantly a certain law of sin that is in his members, that's pulling him down away from God, and about this he must exercise himself constantly, judging it, condemning it, and admitting in the presence of God that in this regard he is not any good in the sight of God. He needs the grace of God.

Romans 8:2 indicates how the Christian can overcome all this because of the Holy Spirit working in him. "For the law of the Spirit of life in Christ Jesus hath made me free from the law of sin and death." In this way Paul is saying, I don't need to fall down because gravity is pulling me down. I can be held up because I've got the strength to walk. In the case of my soul the law of the Spirit of life in Christ Jesus working in me, is stronger: the Spirit "hath made me free from the law of sin and death." Paul goes on to say in verse 8, "So then they that are in the flesh cannot please God." He then goes on to say, "But ye are not in the flesh, but in the Spirit, if so be that the Spirit of God dwell in you." This is to say: You may have the disposition, your body may have the disposition to fall to the ground but you don't have to fall, not as long as you have strength to walk. The Holy Spirit gives you the strength that will hold you up. You can be held up by Him. "Now if any man have not the Spirit of Christ, he is none of his." In other words there is no such thing. That's not the way it's done. The way a human being lives the Christian life is by having Christ in him, having the Holy Spirit working in him. He'll lift him and carry him along.

"And if Christ be in you [if He is actually operative in you], the body is dead because of sin." The Christian can count on this. It is useless to expect human nature to do any differently than it does. "But the Spirit is life because of righteousness." The Christian has something within him that is strong and powerful. "But if the Spirit of him that raised up Jesus from the dead dwell in you, he that raised up Christ from the dead shall also quicken your mortal bodies by his Spirit that dwelleth in you." The Christian has something "going for him" because he belongs to Christ. He has the power of Almighty God by His Holy Spirit working in him that will lift him up: that will deliver him from the bondage of sin. "For if ye live after the flesh, ye shall die: but if ye through the Spirit do mortify the deeds of the body, ye shall live. For as many as are led by the Spirit of God, they are the sons of God." That word "led by the Spirit of God" should not be taken too passively. I could almost have written "as many as are lifted by the Spirit of God, they are the sons of God." "The Spirit itself beareth witness with our spirit, that we are the children of God." This has a profound affect upon the mind because of all that it means.

Paul then goes on to discuss what a wonderful thing it is to know that you're a child of God and that you have God "on your side." "Likewise the Spirit also helpeth our infirmities: for we know not what we should pray for as we ought: but the Spirit itself maketh intercession for us with groanings that cannot be uttered" (Romans 8:26). I have the power of God helping me when I have the Holy Spirit of God in me lifting me into the will of God. No wonder this passage can lead up to this marvelous verse: "And we know that all things work together for good to them that love God, to them who are the called according to his purpose" (Romans 8:28).

We are indebted to Paul for this passage in Romans 7:14-25 describing a person who has the "old man" in him while he is seeking to do the will of God. Then in Chapter 8 Paul shows us how the believer has the Spirit of God in him and can be lifted up. What Paul has said in Romans can be seen again in Philippians 3:4-14. Here is Paul's description of one who is a mature Christian: as long as I live in the flesh, I have my old nature with me, but as long as God is in heaven and Christ Jesus is at the right hand of God and the Holy Spirit has been given unto me, I have the Holy Spirit of God working in me. And so by putting my trust in Him, and looking unto Jesus, "the author and finisher of our faith," and depending on Him, I'm actually helped by the presence of God to overcome the tendencies to turn away, and I'm inclined to walk with Him. What a wonderful thing it is for a Christian to know the living Lord! No wonder the Apostle Paul wanted to "know him, the power of his resurrection, the fellowship of his suffering, being made conformable unto his death; if by any means I might attain unto the resurrection of the dead." This is the constant ambition of the Christian: to be near Christ, trusting in Christ, and have Christ working in him unto victory from day to day.

16.

Conversion

Do you realize that to live as a Christian, a person must start out on a new and different basis?

> Verily I say unto you, Except ye be converted, and become as little children, ye shall not enter into the kingdom of heaven (Matthew 18:3).

I do not think that Jesus of Nazareth was referring to one of our modern evangelistic campaigns, when He said "Except ye be converted." I think He meant something much deeper than that. The word "convert" means turned around, going in a different direction. What He said would mean to us something like this: Except something happens to you that makes you entirely different, and you become as little children, you shall not enter into the kingdom of heaven. In another passage we read that He clearly said: "Ye must be born again."

The "new birth" must make a difference in the person. Nicodemus raised a natural question when he said to Jesus of Nazareth, "How can a man that's forty years old be born again?" He was told not to marvel at that, not to stumble at that. The fact was that he would have to be born again of the Spirit.

We have noted that the Bible speaks of two worlds, this world and the other world: heaven and earth. This world, earth, is limited to time and space. Heaven, which is the spiritual world, is unlimited. In it we move by faith. Every human being lives in the first world. That is where I was born as a baby. That's the natural world, and I came into it as a child of the earth, earthy. My body was composed "of the dust of the earth." The union of father and mother resulted in the natural birth of a child who was a natural person. The Bible teaches that this natural person is sinful. Not all this sin will be ugly, coarse or vulgar. The natural person is interested in self or his satisfaction. He seeks to satisfy himself, in achievement, success or results. This is not like Christ Jesus, who would do nothing for Himself. But you and I put our own desires uppermost and in that we are sinful. Now such a natural person who is interested only in self cannot expect to receive blessing from God.

The blessing of God will come only on someone like His Son, Jesus of Nazareth. "I do always the things which please my Father." If you should wonder where in the world would there be anybody like that I've got news for you: those that are born again, who have Christ in them. Paul writes: "The natural man receiveth not the things of the Spirit of God" (I Corinthians 2:14). It is sobering to realize that every natural person is sinful. But that is exactly what the Bible says.

The natural person can think of the things set forth in the gospel but has no disposition to obey. A natural person can believe there is a God. James says "the devils believe there is one God." As a matter of fact, the Bible says that only the fool says in his heart there is no God. The evidence of God is all around us and is obvious: "The heavens declare the glory of God; and the firmament showeth his handiwork. Day unto day uttereth speech, and night unto night showeth knowledge. There is no speech nor language, where their voice is not heard" (Psalm 19:1-3). That men should believe in God is natural. That men should seek His blessing would be intelligent. But the sin in man's heart turns him away from God. A natural person could accept the Ten Commandments as true, because the Ten Commandments as the written law simply state in so many words what a man's conscience expresses in himself (Romans 2:15). And the natural man could try to obey them. He could realize, "That's the right thing to do, and if I were to do that I would be blessed." But because of sin in his own heart he will not be able to do this.

Isaiah reveals "all our righteousness is as filthy rags." The best man will do is not good enough. The natural person can offer a form of worship. He can go to church and bow down his heart to the idea that God is in that place, and know that here he will come into the presence of God. This may make him feel he is religious.

Saul the Pharisee excelled in the religion of his people far beyond any of his own nation. He lived with a good conscience before God all his days, but he was an unconverted man and was lost in himself. Paul describes this in Philippians 3:3-7 where he says about himself:

> ... have no confidence in the flesh. Though I might also have confidence in the flesh. If any other man thinketh that he hath whereof he might trust in the flesh, I more: circumcised the eighth day, of the stock of Israel, of the tribe of Benjamin, a Hebrew of the Hebrews; as touching the law, a Pharisee; concerning zeal, persecuting the church; touching the right-eousness which is in the law, blameless. But what things were gain to me, those I counted loss for Christ.

We should recognize at this point that each of these things Paul mentioned was good: that he was given to God as a child when his parents circumcised him; that he belonged to the stock of Israel, and that was good; that he was of the tribe of Benjamin and that was good; that he was a Hebrew of the Hebrews and that was good; as touching the law that he was a Pharisee, meaning to say that he believed that the Scriptures of the Old Testament were actually the Word of God and that God inspired them and that was good; concerning zeal he was persecuting the church and was zealous so far as he was concerned; and referring to the righteousness which is in the law, according to the Ten Commandments, he was blameless. Yet Paul himself will tell you, that *he was lost all the time.* Not that any of those things are bad. Actually they "were gain to me." But not one of them was good enough. Not all of them together was good enough. "Those things I count as loss for Christ."

It is important for me as a Christian to read this passage with my eyes open. It may shock me to realize that I could be a preacher, I could be a professor at the Seminary, I could be a Sunday School teacher, I could be a youth worker, I could be a church officer; I could be any of these things and yet not be born again. I can remember the days when I was an unbeliever, when I didn't even believe there was a God, about whom I taught in Sunday School. I believed in the things of the church as a desirable cultural pattern of living. I wanted to help people. Perhaps someone will say, "Well, you were all right then." But I want to say to you, as kindly as I can: No! I was lost! I was in darkness! I was alone! I was on my own! Nobody living can make himself right with God. This is possible only in Christ Jesus. Jesus of Nazareth said plainly: "I am the door; by me if any man enter in," and again: "I am the way, the truth and the life; no man cometh to the Father but by me."

17.

Conviction and Commission

Can you understand why any person who wants to be a strong Christian would need to be totally convinced about some things about God and heaven?

> To whom also he showed himself alive after his passion by many infallible proofs (Acts 1:3).

The first thing Jesus of Nazareth did after He was raised from the dead was to prove to His disciples that He was really alive. The record shows that on the day of the resurrection the disciples were astonished and amazed actually to see Jesus of Nazareth.

We can learn much about growing as a Christian in the record of these early disciples. The life of a Christian begins as he looks into the face of Jesus Christ. But that life is to be nurtured. It actually grows stronger by understanding about Him.

This was demonstrated in the life of Saul the Pharisee, who became Paul the Apostle. We know very little of Saul as a young man, apart from his own writings. We know that he was a young man, very religious and very zealous, and that he was definitely prejudiced against Jesus Christ. We also know that he saw Stephen die, stoned to death as a martyr. He had heard Stephen say, "I see the Son of Man standing at the right hand of God." Later, when Saul was on his way to Damascus to arrest and imprison believers in Jesus Christ, he saw a great light and heard, "Saul, Saul, why persecutest thou me?" The immediate effect upon Saul was to have him say, "Who art thou, Lord?" Then he heard the words, "I am Jesus whom thou persecutest." It was this sight that changed everything in Saul.

For Saul Jesus was dead! But there was no denying the light that shined upon him. But if Jesus were alive, then Saul would have to change his whole mind. This was just what he did. Suddenly he realized that all that Jesus Christ had claimed when He was here upon earth was true: that He was actually the Son of God. Then He actually did die for sinners. And Saul had actually been mistaken. All this truth came to Saul in that blinding flash when God stopped him on the road to Damascus. This same truth had a like effect upon His own disciples after Jesus of Nazareth was raised from the dead, and He had demonstrated that He was risen. He took special care to show them that He was truly, literally, physically raised from the dead! He used "many infallible proofs" including the one saying, "Have you here any food?" Then when they brought Him a piece of broiled fish and a honeycomb, He took it and "did eat before them." This would be proof positive that this was no spirit. This was an actual person, an actual body, right there before them. But even after that remarkable demonstration He spent forty days more, appearing again and again to show them by "many infallible proofs" that He was actually, literally, raised from the dead.

Jesus of Nazareth did this because they needed to know for "sure" so that it could not be explained away. It is just that basic for Christian experience to be convinced of the resurrection of the body. Each of the disciples did not have such an experience as Saul had on the road to Damascus, but during that forty days they had repeated experiences, about which afterwards, over the space of years, they could testify that Jesus of Nazareth was alive. He was their Living Lord. This assurance is of vital importance to this day. Can you take your stand in your home or in your office and say with conviction, Jesus Christ is alive! Can you wake up in the darkness of night in your home and be aware, He is alive! Are you absolutely sure about this?

Conviction that Jesus Christ is alive makes God a living God. I mean just as much alive as I am. It makes Jesus of Nazareth the Son of God, alive now with God in heaven. This makes the resurrection real. He was actually raised from the dead. And this means I'm going to be actually raised from the dead. Each believer is to be actually raised from the dead. (John 5:21-29). If it should happen by some chance that you should die within this next year or the next month, or even the next week, or the next day, would you be able to look death in the face and know that you really are going to be raised from the dead? This would make a difference. You can be assured death would not seem nearly as terrifying. Each person must face death and leaving this world. This conviction that Jesus is alive makes heaven real. It makes the promises of God real.

Before His disciples really could be effectual in the world as witnesses, they needed to be absolutely sure that Jesus of Nazareth was alive. This was essential to their witnessing. The experience of the disciples included seeing Him go up into heaven. Not only was it true that in that forty days' time He showed Himself alive, but on the last day He took them out into the open on a hilltop and there in front of them in full view of them all He ascended into heaven and the cloud received Him out of their sight. You may feel, "That language is strange!" It is! You may think: "I just don't see how that could be." That may be quite possible! But are you going to question it? If you do, you will have to question everything that's in the Bible, because the record says plainly that they did see this. Also there were messengers who came to them and told them: "This same Jesus which you have seen go up into the heavens, shall so come in like manner as you have seen him go."

So for these people, these believers, these Christians—their conviction was that Jesus was alive and that He was coming back. This must be the heart-felt conviction of anyone who wants to share the faith and the life of Christians. It is important to note the disciples were not given any last minute instructions as to how to act. They were not told what they should do about this, or how they should do that; how they should spend their time, or what they should be doing. All those things would be taken care of as they lived. The one thing that could not be taken care of later, the one thing that needed to be absolutely guaranteed to them at the very outset was, that Jesus was alive.

After this conviction had been confirmed they were told, "You shall be witnesses unto me both in Jerusalem, and in all Judea, and in Samaria and unto the uttermost part of the earth." Then they received their commission to be "witnesses unto me." They were to go as "my witnesses." It will be helpful to remember what is expected of a witness on the witness stand. A witness does not explain. In fact, he is not allowed to explain. He is to tell what he has seen and heard. He is to describe. God Himself is invisible. No one can explain Him. His eternal purpose is known to man by reading the Scriptures. The fact that God has raised up Jesus Christ from the dead can be told and the meaning of it can be made plain for us. The disciples were to do this in Jerusalem. I am to do this in my home, in my school, in my office, in my church, among my friends; "and in all Judea," among all my relatives, and all my companions; "and in Samaria," that's among the neighbors who know me. This is to be told everywhere: "and unto the uttermost part of the earth." We have this one fact to tell to all men: Jesus Christ is alive. He is available to you now.

18.

Correction, Communion, Conduct

Can you understand that what a man believes in his heart will really affect the way he lives?

For as he thinketh in his heart, so is he (Proverbs 23:7).

Becoming a Christian takes place inside a person. The message comes from the outside, but it comes into the heart, into the soul. The person learns certain facts that are true. Speaking of myself, this is not anything I do. It is done outside of me. I am a sinner. God is my Judge. God cares about me. God sent His Son for me, and while I was yet a sinner, Christ died for me. Calvary is a reality. The open grave was really there. The ascension into heaven took place just exactly as it reads. Pentecost actually occurred. All those things are outside of me. And if I don't know them I will never be able to be a Christian. But if I know these facts about Jesus Christ I must commit myself to them. The promise of God being with me, of His blessing me and keeping me, is for me. God will send His Holy Spirit into my heart. Since I believe in Christ Jesus, I am to be blessed with the presence of God. This will truly affect me. And I will at once realize there are some things I should do.

What happened to the disciples is written in the book of Acts, mainly in Chapters 1 and 2, and is classic for all Christians. Before the disciples had received the promise from Jesus of Nazareth, He had been with them and had convinced them that He was actually alive, and then in full view of them He ascended into heaven. They were left there by themselves. Then they were told by the messengers that they were to tarry in Jerusalem till they should be endued with power from on high. They returned to Jerusalem and prayed together in an upper room. While they were thus together, they realized things were not right with them. Peter showed the group there was a blemish upon them. There should have been twelve apostles and they now had only eleven. Judas was gone. Immediately they acted to correct what was wrong. They elected a twelfth man.

Any Christian should be prepared to have this happen to him. When we turn ourselves to God, yield ourselves to Him, there would likely be something about us not right; something that does not fit with God's plan. The thing for us to do is to change it and correct it, just as they did. During ten days of prayer, these convinced, corrected people were expectantly waiting for the promise of the Father. In Acts 2:1-13 we can read what actually happened.

> And when the day of Pentecost was fully come, they were all with one accord in one place. And suddenly there came a sound from heaven as of a rushing mighty wind.

We should note this was *"a sound,"* not a wind. "And it filled all the house where they were sitting." Not the wind! The *sound* filled all the house where they were sitting. "And there appeared unto them cloven tongues like as of fire." Again we should note, *not fire!* But *"like as of fire."* "And it sat upon each of them." Not upon just a few chosen ones, but upon everyone.

> And they were all filled with the Holy Ghost, and began to speak with other tongues, as the Spirit gave them utterance. And there were dwelling at Jerusalem Jews, devout men, out of every nation under heaven. Now when this was noised abroad, the multitude came together, and were confounded, because that every man heard them speak in his own language (Acts 2:4-6).

Each who heard could understand the message. That was literally amazing, it was tremendous. It is not surprising to read on: "And they were all amazed, and were in doubt, saying one to another, What meaneth this? Others mocking said, These men are full of new wine." They had heard the disciples speaking, and everyone heard in his own language. Some of the people were astonished and amazed but there were others who laughed at it.

Peter arose and preached his great sermon on the basis of what they saw and what Joel had prophesied (Joel 2:28-32). The record makes it plain that these signs were not for display, but to show that the Holy Spirit had come into the hearts of the believers. The presence of the Holy Spirit makes possible communion with God and with each other. Thus the disciples were all together in one spirit. The life of the believers in the early church in Jerusalem is described in Acts 2:41-47 and presents many significant aspects. "Then they that gladly received his word" is the way their experience started. And that is the way the experience of a Christian always starts. The record goes on to say "they that gladly received the word were baptized." This is the way they made public profession, openly confessing that they believed. "And the same day there were added unto them about three thousand souls. And they continued steadfastly in the apostles' doctrine and fellowship." That means to say they faithfully attended public instruction: preaching was going on and preaching services they attended. "And they continued steadfastly in the apostles' doctrine and fellowship, and in breaking of bread." This refers to their practice of celebrating the Lord's Supper, when they came together faithfully to share in this sacrament. "And in prayers." They attended prayer meetings.

This rich description of the manner of life in the early church showed their faithful worship of God. But there was also a significant result in the way they lived with each other. "And fear came upon every soul": there was a sense of awe and of reverence. "And many wonders and signs were done by the apostles": preaching was powerful and results were obvious. "And all that believed were together": real fellowship prevailed among the believers. They had all things common, sharing unselfishly, "And sold their possessions and goods, and parted them to all men, as every man had need." This indicates brotherly concern. There was mutual aid as needed. This does not say they divided everything they had. They did not put everything into a common fund and then divide it equally. Whenever there was need those that had property shared with those that didn't have it according to their need. "And they, continuing daily with one accord in the temple": they practiced regular attendance in public worship; "and breaking bread from house to house": they had cottage prayer meetings, cottage fellowship meetings. "Did eat their meat with gladness and singleness of heart": there was joy. "Praising God, and having favor with all the people": they enjoyed a good report in the community. "And the Lord added to the church daily such as should be saved." There was joy, praise to God, waiting upon the Lord for increasing and blessing.

19.

The Meaning of Repentance

Can you understand that if a doctor were going to help me, he would first need to diagnose my sickness?

> Come now, and let us reason together, saith the Lord: though your sins be as scarlet, they shall be as white as snow; though they be red like crimson, they shall be as wool. If ye be willing and obedient, ye shall eat the good of the land: but if ye refuse and rebel, ye shall be devoured with the sword: for the mouth of the Lord hath spoken it (Isaiah 1:18-20).

The Christian comes to the Lord in response to His invitation, reasoning together with Him, that he might do His will. Man needs help! He always has and he always will. This is true especially when man has followed his own ideas and gotten into deep trouble. Now God can and does help those who turn to Him; and God will help those who come to Him. Nothing is too hard for God. In the gracious providence of God help is available!

> Behold, the Lord's hand is not shortened, that it cannot save; neither his ear heavy, that it cannot hear: but your iniquities have separated between you and your God, and your sins have hid his face from you, that he will not hear (Isaiah 59:1-2).

God will not endorse sin. He will not smooth over any situation in which there is infection. A doctor would be unworthy if in treating some infection he simply smoothed the top with a band-aid while the infection continued to spread. A faithful doctor would probe and dig that he might be able to remove the cause. God can and will forgive sin if it is confessed. God can cleanse from sin when it is forsaken and God can keep one from sin if it is repudiated, if

80

one's back is turned on it. The whole matter is really very simple and what needs to be done is very plain.

It can happen that a sinner may be unaware of his sin. A poet with true insight into human experience once wrote "Vice is a monster of such dreadful mien, that to be hated needs but to be seen: yet seen too oft', familiar with its face, we first endure, then pity, then embrace." Far too often this is found to be true. I do wrong and I am bothered; I do wrong again, and I am not bothered so much; I do wrong again, and I am hardly bothered at all. The next thing that happens is that I am not even aware of having done wrong. But it is still wrong.

Sometimes this situation occurs in physical matters. Some people have had the bitter experience of going to a doctor for a check-up when they haven't felt well. Following his diagnosis he had advised surgery. When they opened the body they found cancer, undetected, unrecognized.

It is such a common thing when we feel sick to say there is nothing wrong. This is so common the doctor does not trust our feelings nor our words. In my case, he has a thermometer and will measure my temperature. He has a watch with a second hand to count my pulsebeat. He has a stethoscope which he puts on my chest to listen to my heart functioning. He has a device for measuring blood pressure. He wraps it around my arm and looks for various symptoms whereby he is able to detect my physical condition.

Before the coming of the Savior, John the Baptist came to prepare the way of the Lord.

> The voice of him that crieth in the wilderness, Prepare ye the way of the Lord, make straight in the desert a highway for our God. Every valley shall be exalted, and every mountain and hill shall be made low: and the crooked shall be made straight, and the rough places plain: and the glory of the Lord shall be revealed, and all flesh shall see it together: for the mouth of the Lord hath spoken it (Isaiah 40:3-5).

In all this the significance of the highway comes to mind. Isaiah makes this more definite:

> And a highway shall be there, and a way, and it shall be called The way of holiness; the unclean shall not pass over it; but it shall be for those: the wayfaring men, though fools, shall not err therein. No lion shall be there, nor any ravenous beast shall go up thereon, it shall not be found there; but the redeemed shall walk there: and the ransomed of the Lord shall return, and come to Zion with songs and everlasting joy upon their heads: they shall obtain joy and gladness, and sorrow and sighing shall flee away (Isaiah 35:8-10).

John the Baptist preached preparing the way of the Lord by revealing and removing sin. As the doctor has means: his thermometer, stethoscope, and other equipment by which he checks symptoms, so the preacher, John the Baptist had one. It was the law of God. He used the law of God as a mirror that would reveal the sin that was in the human heart. Sin occurs in the human being along the line of a person's actions. Sin develops in our relationship with God, with man and with self. With reference to God, we can forget Him, turn away from Him, forsake Him. With reference to man we can disregard him, ignore him, mistreat him, hurt him; and with reference to self, we can be vain, self-indulgent, self-centered and proud. God sees all these things, and the Word of God is, that God commanded all men everywhere to repent, to acknowledge their sins and to turn away from them to the presence of God.

20.

The Work of Repentance

Do you realize that the first thing any person must do who would become a Christian is to see things as they really are?

Repentance is necessary because of the sin of man. "All have sinned and come short of the glory of God." And wherever there is sin there is need for repentance. Repentance is something that a person does in his own consciousness. It is based upon an honest factual recognition of the situation that he is in. Repentance is not a matter of feeling sorry for past actions. As for myself, often I have a feeling that if I am sorry for what I have done, then I am repenting of it. Such sorrow might be proper enough. It is no doubt true that some of the things that I have done are such that I ought to be sorry about them, but this does not help me. Being sorry for what I have done wrong is like being sorry for water that has gone over the dam; or like crying over spilt milk. How well I can remember that if I had been sent to bring home a pail of milk and on the way I had been careless and I had spilled it, I would certainly have had a good reason for crying. But that would not have gotten the milk back. That is the way it is with reference to being sorry for past actions.

Repenting is not a matter of promising that in the future I'll do better. That would be like my New Year's resolutions. Such promises really do not amount to much.

Repentance then is not a matter of looking back and feeling sorry, or looking ahead and promising to do good. Repentance is looking inward, with an honest appraisal of my own conduct before God. I should keep in mind that as far as God is concerned I am a sinner and that it would be perfectly proper for me to recognize that fact and to depend on Him for His grace and mercy. When I consider that all I have received in providence, all that God has provided: my very life itself and my strength, the circumstances in which I live, the world in which I live in—all this has been given to me. Thus it would be quite right that I should honor God and actually bow down to Him and serve Him. The truth is that in my own selfishness, self-will, and pride, I depend on myself and rebel against God and forsake Him. This is what I need to recognize and confess. God being who He is, and I being who I am, it follows I should worship God.

Because of his sinful heart when the average person recognizes that there is a God, and realizes it would be wise to turn to Him, it is quite natural to worship God with his lips while his heart is far from Him. Man should honor God above all else, and yet oftentimes man worships the work of his own hands: what he does himself, he is inclined to esteem as far more important. God knows the heart of man.

As for me, God knows just exactly how I am full of myself; and He will not hear me when I pray. Thinking only of myself, I am out of touch with God. In the matter of other people I have a responsibility to them all. God in His righteousness can ask me point blank: "Where is thy brother? What's your attitude toward other people?" If it turns out that I have shared in oppressing those that are weaker than I am; or if I have been unfair, quarrelsome and contentious, God will know my conduct and will not endorse evil. As long as I am that kind of a person, I need not expect the blessing of God, for I will not get it.

God sees people as they are. He sees the vanity of their human attitudes. This can be seen in the apparel some people wear, in the self-indulgence to be seen among men, in the tendency to drunkenness and addictions of one kind and another. The self-centeredness of some people leads into immorality. Even in those who do not do anything outwardly wrong to anybody, there is often a lack of charity and love toward the crying needs of others. This can be seen in the attitude of the Levite in the parable of the Good Samaritan. Thus they also ignore the needs of others and walk by on the other side; or they are like the priest in that parable, in that they do not want to become involved.

Also, there is the emptiness and the dimness of the soul, the darkness that one feels and the anguish that one has because he is all alone. All these things God knows. He knows the pride of the human heart, and He resisteth the proud. Because all this is true, it is essential that man should come before God and admit his own sinfulness.

Luke records how John the Baptist in preaching to the people in his day and time, pointed out to them that they should bring forth fruits meet for repentance. They should show in their conduct that they actually had repented: "Bring forth therefore fruits worthy of repentance" (Luke 3:8). These fruits that He asks for are not repentance. Repentance is the attitude I have in my own heart, but the actions God wants to see are to be worthy as evidence that my attitude is genuine.

First John the Baptist pointed out conditions that would hinder true repentance. Some people do not want to acknowledge that they are sinners. They do not want to admit openly that they are wrong, because they claim they belong to a group of Christians. Perhaps they belong to a certain church; or perhaps their family belongs to that church. John the Baptist would say to such people: "Begin not to say within yourselves, We have Abraham to our Father."

At this point John the Baptist says something further: "And now also the axe is laid unto the root of the trees: every tree therefore which bringeth not forth good fruit is hewn down, and cast into the fire" (Luke 3:9). In this way he was telling the people that repentance was necessary because God would cut down any tree that was barren. This simply means that if in my own life I live in such a way that I'm out of touch with God, so that I am not producing the kind of results that are glorifying to God, then I'm like a barren tree and can only look forward to being cut down in the judgment of God.

John the Baptist then applied his preaching to show three different kinds of fruit that would be worthy.

> And the people asked him, saying, What shall we do then? He
> answereth and saith unto them, He that hath two coats, let
> him impart to him that hath none; and he that hath meat, let
> him do likewise (Luke 3:10-11).

After a man had repented and sincerely confessed himself to be a
sinner, he would act in a way that would be different from his
natural sinfulness. Instead of being covetous and selfish he would be
generous and charitable to others.

> Then came also publicans to be baptized, and said unto him,
> Master, what shall we do? And he said unto them, Exact no
> more than that which is appointed you (Luke 3:12-13).

The publicans were tax gatherers, and when they asked, What
would be action on our part that would be worthy of repentance?
He said, "Be fair. Don't take advantage of anybody."

> And the soldiers likewise demanded of him, saying, And what
> shall we do? And he said unto them, Do violence to no man,
> neither accuse any falsely; and be content with your wages
> (Luke 3:14).

Thus to the soldiers the Lord pointed out the very area in which
they might act naturally.

All three examples showed the need for a new attitude. Jesus of
Nazareth plainly taught "You must be born again." This means the
believer must be entirely changed to be a new creature in Christ
Jesus.

Repentance opens the way for the new birth. When admitting
deep down in my heart that I am not what I ought to be, then I am
ready to obey His call. The result will be that I act differently.

> Therefore if any man be in Christ, he is a new creature: old
> things are passed away; behold, all things are become new (II
> Corinthians 5:17).

21.

The Result of Repentance

Can you see how being honest with myself about my own inner thoughts and attitudes helps me to arrive at a peace of mind and heart?

> But if we walk in the light, as he is in the light, we have fellowship one with another, and the blood of Jesus Christ his Son cleanseth us from all sin (I John 1:7).

This wonderful promise is for all who will humbly and sincerely respond to the call of God. "If we walk in the light": if we will admit openly, honestly, candidly, just what we are; "as he is in the light, we have fellowship one with another, and the blood of Jesus Christ his Son cleanseth us from all sin"; we would be blessed with all the blessing of a full salvation. By the grace of God working in our hearts, repentance is a personal attitude and action that we take about ourselves. And so when I repent I do something in me about me.

There are things about the gospel that we share in knowledge with other people, and there are things that we share in esteem with other people. We honor God because others honor God. We understand about heaven because others understand about heaven. We desire that our souls should be saved because we understand from others that this can be done in Christ Jesus. It is always impressive to one's heart that other people believe in God.

With all its faults and failings, Christianity is impressive. About 1900 years ago in this world a few people in an obscure province of the Roman Empire, led by the Holy Spirit of God, started this whole movement. They had no country of their own. They were just a few

Jews to whom the Roman Empire paid very little attention. Yet among those people a small handful of folks started out with a gospel message which they aimed to take to the whole wide world. This they did! Starting from there since then that message has spread until it has gone around the world.

The personal testimony of many, many significant persons as well as that of the most downtrodden who have been blessed by believing the gospel is impressive. This is something that has not been done in a corner. Important men and important women in the course of history believed in the Lord Jesus Christ. Even today any number of great men don't mind letting it be publicly known that they believe in God the Father, and God the Son, and God the Holy Spirit. I know not everybody does, but many people do, and that is impressive.

The general testimony of the history of the Christian church throughout all generations also cannot be totally discounted. To be sure there are many things about the church that are open to question, and in a good many ways its record is by no means perfect; but when all is said and done history shows that things have happened in the name of the Gospel, in the name of Jesus Christ on the face of the earth, in a way that is literally marvelous. The results in the record are fantastic, and yet there is still a more important line of truth that indicates the power of the gospel.

To be effectual the gospel truth must be applied in the individual. In the sacrament of the Lord's Supper a number of professing believers can sit in a group and have the sacraments administered to them. The officers will carry the trays around and offer the bread and the cup to the people who are there to worship. Regardless of the number that are there on a given day, what makes that service actually meaningful to me is that I swallow the bread down my own throat: that goes to me; and I drink that cup down my own throat: that goes to me. It is just so with repentance.

Repentance is an exercise of recognition in the individual's consciousness. It is a matter of my recognizing and confessing things as they are. I must see the truth about me as I am. I must see the truth about me as I am in the presence of God. I must show the truth that I know as I live, this must be recognized and confessed in me. The Scriptures will serve as a mirror. I look into them, and they show me what is true inside of me. In the light of that word, the Bible, I see that as a human being I have turned away from God: I have forsaken God. Although I didn't create myself and I didn't create this world, I live in the world as though I owned it. I walk around in this world as if it were all mine. I take anything I want and leave anything I like and do as I please, just as if I were the only person living in the world.

Do you realize that there are many people who will get up this morning, and live this day and go to bed tonight, who will not give God a second thought? Every bit of air they breathe, He made it. Every single pulse beat that was in their body, He gave them strength for it. Every person they met, He provided. Every single thing that happened He has watched over and knows about.

And when I am a party in that sort of conduct don't you realize He knows this is true about me? When I consider how it is with me and other people: how I've neglected to help those that were in need; how I've avoided people who were in trouble when I didn't want to become involved; how I drew my skirts about me and went my way because I had my own business to do—don't you know He has seen all that? And when I have seen how I have flattered myself from time to time thinking of my own importance; and how I feel about things which I claim for my own, I realize how the Word of God will judge me to be a sinner in His sight.

The Bible shows me how I really am. If I'm willing to admit the truth, if I'm willing to confess it, and say openly before God that I am a sinner, I am on the way to blessing. The Scriptures show me I'm just not fit for the presence of God nor to receive His blessing. This is recorded about other people in the Bible. Job said,

> I have heard of thee with the hearing of the ear, but now mine eyes seeth thee, and I abhor myself in dust and ashes.

Isaiah was a good man, but he said about himself:

> I am a man of unclean lips; I dwell in the midst of a people of unclean lips. Mine eyes have seen the glory of the Lord.

Paul the Apostle was a man who could say that he had lived all his life in good conscience before God and had profited in the Jews' religion far beyond any of his own age, yet he said about himself, "I know that in me, (that is in my flesh) there dwelleth no good thing."

The full result of repentance is shown in that man who was praying in the Temple and durst not so much as lift up his face unto God, but could only say, "God be merciful to me a sinner."

Repentance is an exercise that penetrates to the very heart of a man and cleanses him. Repentance clears the way for fellowship with the Father and with other Christians. For myself, having once and for all plainly admitted that I am a sinner, I do not need to be discouraged because the Word of God tells me I have an advocate with the Father, even Jesus Christ the righteous. Becoming a Christian is not by reason of my works, nor because I'm that good; but I am going to be saved and blessed by His righteousness, by His grace and by His Spirit.

The matter of becoming a Christian is like getting to the tenth floor of a building, not by walking the stairs but by riding the elevator. When I get into the elevator and go up to the tenth floor, I'm not any stronger than I was when I was on the first floor. The elevator took me up. If I get across the lake in a boat which uses a motor; the motor takes me across the lake, it is not that I am a good paddler. It is not that I am able to row across the lake; the motor took me over. This is the way it is with reference to the blessing of God. Repentance opens the door. The Lord comes in and I am saved by Him. To be sure that is humbling, but that is good; because now I am saved and that is glorious. Now I can rejoice in the Lord, and I am able to walk with Him to the glory of God. For now Christ liveth in me by His grace and by His mercy.

22.

The Meaning of Believing

Do you think a person could be intelligent and believe in the reality of something he has never seen?

"The just shall live by faith." "But without faith it is impossible to please him: for he that cometh to God must believe that he is and that he is a rewarder of them that diligently seek him." "According to thy faith be it unto thee." These words chosen at random out of the New Testament emphasize something that is well known to everyone who understands or has ever heard the gospel. Those who are saved are saved by faith. To be a Christian is a matter of believing the gospel, but what does it mean to believe?

Believing is something I do: I believe. It is an action on my part in my consciousness. Believing is a good deal like swallowing. As a matter of fact, it is so implied in our language. If you were to overhear someone telling an account of what he has done, which may sound rather impossible or exaggerated, you might ask the person next to you, "Can you swallow that?" We would all know what you meant: "Can you believe that to be true?" Swallowing does not make anything right, or true, or clean. Swallowing is an action on my part in which I take in food. Swallowing food would nourish the body, but swallowing poison would be fatal to the body. But the swallowing in both cases would be the same. Some poisons look just like milk. If the substance were in a glass you couldn't tell which it is. That is why we must be so careful with reference to food. Mistakes are possible.

And this is true also in the matter of believing. In the matter of faith, errors are possible. Mistakes are possible. Consider swallowing again. Several years ago a tragic incident occurred in a hospital in this country. While a nurse was preparing food for children in the babies' ward in the hospital, she took a certain ingredient, which she thought was a baby's formula, and put it in the food which she gave to the babies. The babies became sick and eight of them died, because what she mistook for a baby's formula was actually a bottle of detergent. She thought it was a baby's formula. In this she was genuinely sincere. But the babies died. The fact that the babies swallowed the preparation did not make it food. The fact that the nurse gave it to them as if it were food did not make it safe.

In dealing with spiritual things someone may say, "I don't think it makes any difference what you believe, just so you believe." That's exactly like saying it doesn't make any difference what you swallow, just so you swallow. Wouldn't believing be sufficient guarantee in any case? No! You must believe according to knowledge. You need to understand about it in order for it to be safe. Someone will say, "Well, I think if you're sincere, that's all that's required." Now being sincere is no safeguard. I can assure you that that unfortunate nurse, that poor young woman, was entirely sincere that morning when she prepared those baby formulas. That didn't help any.

Believing, no matter how sincere or how earnest I may be, commits me to the consequences of what I am believing. If I am believing something that's true, then the consequences can be good. But if I believe something that's false then the consequences will be evil. Anybody with experience in business will know exactly what is meant. When thinking of people cheating one another in business, there is no time when one is as readily cheated as when trusting a man, taking him at his word. Someone may say, "It follows from all this that a person just shouldn't believe anything. It would be wise to doubt everything."

In my own experience this was the way it was with me. I grew up into manhood with a general frame of mind in which I thought it was an intelligent thing to doubt. As a matter of fact I felt that if you were smart you would doubt. I am inclined to think there are people who still have that same idea. I remember my frame of mind when I was thinking that it was intelligent to doubt. I doubted the Bible, and so I wouldn't read it: I simply turned away in continuing unbelief.

At this point my personal experience turned when I began to doubt my doubts. I asked myself why was I so sure I was right, when I was doubting? Why not examine this? I outlined a simple procedure. At that time I was boarding at a certain farm home where I was teaching school. I asked myself, How do I know when I sit down to the table in the morning and my hostess brings scrambled eggs for breakfast and serves me that they are safe? Could I not doubt they are pure? Has she had them examined? Couldn't they be poisoned? How would I know by looking at them? Now if it is intelligent to doubt, why not doubt that?

In the same way, suppose someone were coming to take me somewhere in a car, and before I got in the car I'd ask this person, "Have you checked your steering wheel? Have you looked at it since the last time you drove so that you can be real sure it's not broken?" And again, supposing that as I was about to enter an elevator I were to stop at the elevator door and ask the operator, "Have you had your cable checked? Are you real sure the cable will take you to the top of this building? Do you know for sure it won't break?" Suppose someone handed me some money in change as I bought something, and in it was a $5 bill. Suppose I took this $5 bill and holding it up to the storekeeper I would say, "Have you had this checked as to whether it is counterfeit? Have you had this taken by the bank to see if it's okay?" I continued to think and to turn these things over in my mind because that was exactly what I was doing with the Bible. I began to have a very queer feeling that if I actually did those things, people would be out looking for me with a net. It would mean that I was crazy as a loon.

I continued to reflect on the intelligence of doubting. In turning that over in my mind, I considered what would happen if I were going to a doctor. Suppose that I needed to go for an examination for a life insurance policy. The doctor would ask me to stick out my tongue. He would take my blood pressure. He would listen to my heartbeat with a stethoscope. I would have no idea what opinion he was forming in his own mind. After he had done all those things he would ask me some questions which I would answer. Then he would write out a prescription. Even if I looked at it, I wouldn't understand it. It would look like a lot of hieroglyphics, just short abbreviations. I would take this prescription to a drug store to secure the medicine it prescribed. The druggist would look at it and then go back into the back part of the drug store where there would be a thousand bottles of all kinds, many of them containing various kinds of poison. After awhile he would come out with some capsules and hand them to me in a box. But would I know what was in those capsules? No, but would I take them? Yes, I'd follow the directions. And why would I take them? Because I would have good sense. Because I would be intelligent. It is intelligent to believe on sufficient evidence.

It did not take me long to realize that when it comes to believing in God, I could go out and look: "the heavens declare the glory of God; the firmament showeth his handiwork." I could look around about me and see all these things which God has made. I could open the Bible and read the Word of God. I could think of all the people who have believed in Him. Then I could ask myself, wouldn't I be safe if I trusted in Him?

23.

Believing and Obedience

Do you realize that believing in God will cause a change in a person's way of living?

> By faith Abraham, when he was called to go out into a place which he should after receive for an inheritance, obeyed; and he went out, not knowing whither he went (Hebrews 11:8).

Believing in God means much more than believing that God exists. It includes that, as it includes conviction in the reality of God; but it also includes confidence in the will of God as revealed in the Word of God. When I say I believe, I mean I take something invisible to be true and real, something that I haven't seen, something that I don't have in hand, but something I have heard about which I now take to be true and real. This is what I mean when I say I believe. Believing deals with things that are not present and not visible.

"Faith" can be used in connection with matters of knowledge. For instance I can say, "I believe it is five miles to the post office." That can actually be checked, and whether or not I'm right or wrong can be proven by just watching the speedometer of the car. Or I can say, "I believe that sack weighs ten pounds." I can put it on the scale and find out. The term "faith" can be used in referring to matters of fact and of knowledge that can be put to the test. But when used in the gospel, speaking about believing in the Lord Jesus Christ, "faith" is used in connection with things that are invisible. "Faith is the substance of things hoped for, the evidence of things not seen."

Sometimes a person may say, "I'm going to believe only what I can see." This is actually not practical. Consider what you see when you look down a railroad track running straight away from you. The rails seem to be coming together. Yet you know perfectly well that is not true, even though that is what you saw. Or take the example of seeing a pencil in a glass half filled with water. It will seem that the pencil is broken in the middle. This will demonstrate that you actually do not believe what you see.

A person can believe and take as being true something that he has not seen, but which has been experienced by others. Let us suppose I am driving across the country in my car and come to a canyon, over which there is a suspension bridge. It looks rather frail to me. I want to go across, but I wonder if that bridge will hold me? Let us say I am sitting in my car by the side of the road trying to decide whether to risk driving over it. A man with a big gravel truck comes along, stops, and calls down to me, "What's the matter? Having trouble?" I tell him, "I need to get across that river; I need to get over that canyon, but I'm not sure that bridge will hold me." The man might say, "Oh, sure, it'll hold you. It'll be all right." I might say to him, "How do you know? Are you an engineer?" "No, but I take this truck over-filled with gravel. I go over it every day. That bridge will hold you." This would be good evidence. On the basis of that I can drive on that bridge. That is to say I can believe that the bridge will hold me up. Why can I now believe? Because someone who had gone over that bridge told me it was reliable.

A person can put confidence in medicine, doctors and hospitals when other people testify they were helped. This is actually intelligent. This is how we can benefit by the experience of other people. On one occasion I was present at a service club luncheon where I was to give a talk. I was there ahead of time and the lady who acted as Secretary of this club came in to arrange the flowers on the tables. Thus we met each other. The lady said, "You're the speaker today?" I said, "Yes, ma'am." Later she asked me, "Who wrote Genesis?" I told her, "I don't know. I know that tradition says that Moses wrote it. The New Testament refers to it as the writings of Moses. Jesus of Nazareth referred to quotations from it as something that Moses had written. As far as I'm concerned, I believe Moses wrote it, but I wasn't there. I didn't see him do it." She stopped in amazement: "You don't know who wrote it?" I said, "No, ma'am. I accept tradition, but I really don't know." "Yet you believe it?" I said, "Yes, ma'am." She said, "Isn't that funny?" "Yes," I said, "I guess that's funny, but I'm kind of a funny person." Reaching into my pocket, I took out a bottle of capsules I had just purchased at a drug store. I said, "Here is a bottle of some capsules I just bought at the drug store. The doctor instructed me to take one of these before each meal. And that is what I am going to do, even though I do not know the name of the druggist that made them up." She looked at me. I repeated, "I don't know the name of the druggist that made up these capsules, but I am going to take them. I'm funny that way." She didn't ask me any more questions.

Could I believe the Bible even if I didn't know who was the author of every book? As a matter of fact, I could treat it very much like medicine. What does the Bible claim to do? It claims to bring peace. Medicine claims to bring health. The Bible claims to bring salvation. Has anyone ever tried it? As a matter of fact, many people have tried it. What do they say? They say it works. This is what the missionaries say when they take it to the mission field. This is what the evangelists say when they preach it on the public platform. This is what the pastors say when they go into the homes. This is what the Christians say when they read their Bibles. They all say this is actually the Word of God that blesses the soul. Should I then doubt it? I will take it the way they take it and I will try it out; when I have tried it out I will say I know.

If you planned to meet a friend on Tuesday afternoon at three o'clock at the post office, and he agreed to that plan, what would you expect to do? Would you not expect on Tuesday afternoon to go to the post office and meet the friend? How would you know he would be there? Could you tell it by looking at him? Could you tell it by what he was wearing? Then how could you know you would meet him at three o'clock on Tuesday afternoon at the post office? Because he said so. You had his promise and you believed his promise and so you expected to meet him. So it is with believing the

Bible. It is the promise of God and when you have it and you believe it, you will trust it.

Such believing is the very basis of Christian experience.

> While we look not at the things which are seen, but at the things which are not seen: for the things which are seen are temporal; but the things which are not seen are eternal (II Corinthians 4:18).

Because God is a living Being and has a will of His own, believing in Him can mean that I will be called on to act according to what He wants me to do. Abraham believed in God. God said, "Get thee out of thy father's country." Abraham went. Naaman the Syrian who was a leper believed in God as Elisha told him to wash in the Jordan seven times. When he obeyed and washed seven times, "his flesh came again like unto the flesh of a little child." Peter at the lakeside heard the Lord Jesus saying, "Launch out and let down your nets for a draught of fish." Peter himself apparently did not think there was anything to be gained by going, but the Lord told him to do it, so he obeyed. He got more fish than he could handle. Martha standing at the grave of Lazarus told the Lord Jesus that Lazarus had been dead four days. The Lord said to her, "Take ye away the stone." Because she believed in Him, she did take away the stone and Lazarus was raised from the dead. So in believing God we obey Him and this is what brings the blessing of God.

24.

Believing and Blessing

Have you understood that all that a believer needs to do to have the blessing of God is to accept it when it is offered?

"Abraham believed God and it was counted to him for righteousness." That's the way the Bible puts it. The heart of the gospel is that the living God saves His people, blesses His people. A common error in the matter of living in the presence of God and having the blessing of God, is to hold that man qualifies for this by his own works. This may be because man is proud, and thinks he can do it himself. When his heart is dark with unbelief, a man does not think God will do it for him. Someone has to do so, and so he tries it, but this is the mistake. There is one truth that is openly declared in the Bible repeatedly: "By the works of the law shall no flesh be justified." The Scriptures teach plainly salvation is a free gift to the glory of God. And that really means that if you and I are going to be saved, God is going to do it. The living God is able and He is ready to win, to save and to keep those who put their trust in Him.

Jesus of Nazareth taught it plainly when He was here. "I am the door; by me if any man enter in he shall be saved." "I am the way, the truth and the life. No man cometh to the Father, but by me." The invitation that He gave to the whole world promised everything that we're talking about: "Whosoever believeth in me shall never perish but have everlasting life." And this was true because He, Jesus Christ the Son of God, would "make it good." On my part, I only believe; I take what God promises as true; I live in it, and God will make it real through Jesus Christ.

Believing is not a matter of my pushing my own ideas. When the Bible uses the word believing, it means the believer is depending upon the will of God as revealed in His Word in His promises. Believing enables the believer to receive God's promises in place of his own ideas. It is never a matter of the believer doing the best he can. Even a Christian can be tempted to do that. I can sympathize with the person who says, "I'm going to change my ways." I could ask him, "What are you going to do?" "I'm going to do better." "What do you mean?" "From now on I'm going to do my very best." I could even ask him, "Why?" He might answer, "I want the blessing of God. And because I want the blessing of God I'm going to do my very best. I'm quite sure if I do my very best God will bless me." That person is mistaken! God does not promise that He will bless the person who is doing his very best. God will bless the soul that obeys Him and trusts Him.

Suppose a ship were sinking and a lifeboat went out to rescue passengers and crew. In the event that a man is taken up out of the sea and put in the boat, that man can now expect to get to shore. How? By swimming? Shall he swim around in the bottom of the boat to get to shore? This sounds ridiculous and it is. The way that man will get to shore is to stay in that boat. The boat will take him to shore. So it is in the gospel. Paul states it plainly, "But to him that worketh not, but believeth on him that justifieth the ungodly, his faith is counted for righteousness" (Romans 4:5). I will never get to heaven because I am doing so well. I will get there by the grace of God because He will take me there. I will not be able to do this because I am such a smart person. The Lord will do it for me, because He is gracious.

Human pride will prompt a man to try and save himself. Many persons seem to think, "I'd be glad to have the Lord forgive me everything I've done in the past, and if He will do that, I think I can make it from here on." Foolish man! He could not do God's will in the past, and he will not be able to do it the rest of the way. Humility would help the man to accept God's provision. Back of all the blessing promised in salvation is the power of God. Any Christian person can truthfully say of himself, "I am saved by the power of God."

Believing in some respects works very much like radar. I recall some years ago it was my privilege to fly home from the Philippine Islands. I boarded an airplane in Manila and we flew across to Los Angeles, by way of Honolulu. On the way we were to stop in the middle of the Pacific at a small spot called Wake Island. From away up there in the sky where we were flying it seemed we were aiming to come down on a small sand bar in the middle of the Pacific Ocean. I had all the confidence in the crew and in the plane but there were moments when I couldn't help but think we were doing a mighty risky thing. How could we do this? Because of instruments the crew had that used radar. Using such means we were able to fly down, right to that island, landing exactly on the landing strip at just the right level, at just the right height, and in the right place.

The whole procedure involves not only the crew on the plane but also a crew at the landing field. The crew at the landing field can see this plane coming miles and miles away. They guide the pilot using their instruments on the ground by electronic means sending messages to him in the plane. The pilot watching his screen in front of him, while sitting in his cockpit can actually see himself being guided along. He is guided to fly in a certain way, so much to the right, so much to the left, so much up, so much down, as he makes his approach. It is the ground crew that brings him in at just the right height, at just the right speed. This illustration sets forth the likeness of a Christian's walk.

While the Christian is living in this world his landing strip is in heaven. Though as a believer I am living in this world, I'm going home to heaven, and the "landing crew" up there in heaven, headed by the Lord Jesus Christ, has me in sight all my life long. Through the Holy Spirit, my Lord is able to share with me the guidance of God. Thus by faith I can actually be led so that I am doing what God wants me to do here on earth, and so He is bringing me right in on His airstrip. Heaven is my home airstrip. The ground crew that is guiding me is up there in heaven. While I'm riding along here in this world, by faith, I can see it afar, and with confidence I can move right along into that heavenly landing field.

In due time the believer can settle into the arms of his Heavenly Father. Radar doesn't put the airstrip out there. Radar didn't put Wake Island down there in the Pacific Ocean, and doesn't move Wake Island around. Radar guides the pilot just as the grace of God moves the believer around to bring him in line to land home with the Lord. It is a marvelous thing that all the blessing of God is available because God graciously wants to save us by His grace and mercy. All we need to do is yield ourselves into His will and obey Him.

25.

The Meaning of Receiving

Do you know what a person must do to have the Holy Spirit working in the heart?

> And when he had said this, he breathed on them, and saith unto them, Receive ye the Holy Ghost (John 20:22).

The Christian gospel opens the way for any man to receive the blessing of God. It is so natural for us to think that in order to receive the blessing of God we must *do something.* We feel that we ought to make ourselves worthy of it. But we need to recognize that it is God that saves the soul. It is God that saves the person. Salvation is not something a man does by following a good example. This is not something that a person achieves within himself by good effort.

One of man's biggest snares is pride and he can be misled in pride as a result of his ignorance about, or unbelief in, God's plan. Man needs the blessing of God. In his ambition and pride he wants to do something big enough for it so that he can feel that is something he earned. In dealing with God we need to learn clearly and plainly "except ye be as little children you shall not enter the kingdom of heaven." Wouldn't you say about "little children" that they're dependent? No one expects them to do anything for their living. This is the plain meaning of the Scripture, "except ye be as little children." As a believer you are to receive from God what He is going to give you, just the way a baby receives from it's mother what the baby needs.

Paul makes this clear when he writes to the Galatians:

> But when the fullness of the time was come, God sent forth

his Son, made of a woman, made under the law, to redeem
them that were under the law, that we might receive the
adoption of sons. And because ye are sons, God hath sent
forth the Spirit of his Son into your hearts, crying, Abba,
Father (4:4-6).

Notice two things God did: in verse 4 "God sent forth his Son" and
in verse 6 "God hath sent forth the Spirit of his Son." He sent forth
His Son to redeem; and He sent forth the Holy Spirit into your
hearts crying Abba, Father. Thus what needs to be done in the
salvation of our souls has been done in Christ Jesus: He is the Savior.
If I'm going to have salvation I will receive it from Him. To be sure I
must appropriate it; I must receive it; I must take it; but God
provides it. God sent Christ Jesus to do what was necessary for us.
He was to do what was needed; and He is right now doing what is
needed; and He will do whatever will be needed in the days to come.
"But as many as received him, to them gave he power to become the
sons of God, even to them that believe on his name" (John 1:12).

This can be understood in a very simple way if you will think
about a lady acting as hostess. She prepares a tray of sandwiches and
takes them to her guests. That gesture on her part, offering that tray
of sandwiches to me, implies she made those sandwiches to make
them available to me. She held them before me and invited me to
take one, knowing that if I would take it I would have it. What is the
simple meaning of this? I will get just as much off that tray as I take.
This is the way it is with the Lord, and this is how it is with the
gospel.

It is important to learn that in receiving things from God, I accept
His offer and trust in His power. It is like being on a lake, when the
boat I've been riding in capsizes and I am floundering around in the
lake trying to keep from drowning, and a man comes by with a
lifeboat. He calls to me: "Get in the boat." When I get in the boat, I
can stop struggling and relax, the boat will take me to shore.

Consider another simple illustration: how do I get to the tenth
floor of a building? I could climb the stairs, or I could get into the

elevator. If I step into the elevator; the door will be shut and the elevator will take me up ten floors. I then get out on the tenth floor. Am I tired? No! Am I out of breath now? No! How did I get there? The elevator took me there. But I did not do it. The elevator did it for me. Being a Christian is like that.

The same verb used by the Holy Spirit to say God "sent forth" His Son was used to say God "sent forth" His Holy Spirit into my heart. God does it, and apparently this has been done in every believer. You and I would certainly agree that when Christ Jesus died, He died for all men. He died for all sinners. Now I ask you quickly, are they all saved? And you will say: "No, the Scripture says 'As many as received him, to them gave he power to become the Sons of God.' " True! Now God sent forth the Spirit of His Son into the hearts of the believers. Are they all going to have the Spirit operative? The truth of the matter is: only those who receive Him. I must receive Him. That raises a question. How can I receive Him if He's already in my heart? Let me illustrate it for you like this: suppose a lady in her home was expecting at some time during the day that a distinguished guest was coming to stay with her. At a certain time during the day word comes in from the front room that the guest is already in the house. If the guest is already in the house, because some servant or some child let the guest come into the house, what must the hostess do? The hostess must go and *receive* that guest. She doesn't have to bring him in from the outside. He's already in. But she is to receive him, to acknowledge his presence, and to appreciate his person. She must treat him with honor and esteem which is his due. She must extend to him the courtesies of welcome. God has already put the Holy Spirit in my heart. What I must do now is: receive Him. I must recognize His presence. John reports a very significant promise:

> And I will pray the Father, and he shall give you another Comforter . . . Even the Spirit of truth; whom the world cannot receive, because it seeth him not, neither knoweth him (John 14:16-17).

The world cannot receive the Spirit because it doesn't see Him and

doesn't know Him. When we use the word "see" we mean "understand": because the world does not understand Him, it cannot
receive Him. The word "know" means "to appreciate"; because the
world does not know Him nor esteem Him it cannot receive Him.
Apparently if I am ignorant of the Holy Spirit, and indifferent to
Him as the Person of God, because I do not appreciate Him, this will
disqualify me. The person who wants to grow and to mature as a
Christian needs to meditate upon this truth. The Holy Spirit must be
understood for what He will do and His presence must be appreciated for who He is or He cannot operate in that soul. That soul will
not be blessed with the work of the Holy Spirit of God.

26.

The Baptism of the Holy Spirit

Do you understand what is meant by the sacrament of baptism in the Christian church?

"Repent, and be baptized every one of you in the name of Jesus Christ for the remission of sins, and ye shall receive the gift of the Holy Ghost" (Acts 2:38). These are the words spoken by the Apostle Peter to the multitude on the day of Pentecost, when they asked, "Men and brethren, what shall we do?" The practice of baptism as a ceremony involving the use of water has always been employed in the course of evangelism, the preaching of the Christian gospel. There are definite and different opinions about the significance, meaning and practice of this sacrament. But there is truth revealed in the record which is basic for all views on the baptism of the Holy Spirit, which will help the reader to learn what the Bible really teaches.

Baptism as such seems to be a spiritual operation affecting the soul. This is an external ceremony. A practice in which water is used, which symbolizes the real operation. This does not mean that the water itself is actually involved in the operation affecting the soul. Consider the other sacrament, the Lord's Supper. When the minister says, "This is my body broken for you," there are few today in the Protestant church who feel that the bread is actually the body of Jesus Christ. It seems obvious that it is used as a symbol. When Christ Jesus took that bread and broke it, He was pointing to the time when His body on Calvary would be broken. Bread is available everywhere; and when the Lord Jesus took bread in His hands and breaking it said, "This is my body broken for you. Take, eat. This do in remembrance of me," He was instituting a memorial to celebrate something very important. Something very significant was to happen and this ceremony shows it.

Repeating the ceremony is helpful, and believers are urged to share in the sacrament of the Lord's Supper, by being present when it is celebrated and sharing in it by actually partaking of the bread and the cup. It can be noted there are various practices used in celebrating the sacrament of the Lord's Supper. In the matter of the bread, where the language of the Scripture states, "This is my body broken for you," it seems clear that He took the loaf of bread and broke it with His hands to share it with the people. Despite the plain way this was described many people today partake of the Lord's Supper by having bread served in little squares that have been cut ahead of time. Some denominations use wafers. No one seems offended by this change in procedure. The idea is clearly the same in all the practices. It is always bread that is used. This same is true with the cup. When He said to them, "This cup is the New Testament in my blood," the word "cup" was in the singular. But today when the Lord's Supper is celebrated, there are usually cups, trays of little cups that are used. Thus the mode of dispensing the cup has varied, but the truth has been the same all the way through. And when He said as He held that cup, "This cup is the New Testament in my blood," it is understood that that cup did not contain the actual physical blood of Jesus Christ. The blessing to my soul when I partake of that celebration of the Lord's Supper, when I eat the bread even though it is cut in little squares ahead of time, and I drink the cup even though it is served to me in a single cup all of my own, is not in the way the bread is served, and in the way the wine is served, the blessing is derived because of the *truth that is involved.* His body was broken for me, His blood was shed for me. Now my soul is blessed when I remember that, and that blessing is not dependent on any mode that may be employed.

The outstanding classic demonstration of baptism was practiced by John the Baptist. John the Baptist did not invent baptism. He did not initiate it. But he used it with a special significance. Apparently baptism was used among the people of that time to indicate acceptance of the message that had been heard. When the preaching was willingly received, when the person listening said, "I'll accept that because that is what I think," his acceptance would be indicated to anyone seeing him being baptized with water.

The idea can be seen in the case of a young man courting a young girl. As they become engaged, he gives her a ring by putting it on her finger. The ring is a token. It indicates that she accepted his proposal.

Something like this happens when people come forward to be baptized. When a pastor or an evangelist preaches, an invitation is given. Anyone who accepts what is being preached comes forward. This coming forward on his part indicates that he has accepted what has been preached. Thus his baptism illustrates, celebrates, the fact that the preacher has communicated the gospel to this man and he has received it.

The doctrine of baptism in various churches is confusing as the mode in baptism is uncertain. The New Testament does not describe the mode. Reading every instance of it will not show how the water was used. Earnest Christians have arrived generally at two different modes. But the result is the same. When a person has listened to the preaching and accepted the message, when he has accepted the call and wants to openly identify himself with the name of the Lord Jesus Christ in public, he comes forward to be baptized the way that particular preacher will baptize him. In the other sacrament of the Lord's Supper the mode was set out quite clearly. Believers have changed that mode according to their own ideas of what was suitable to them. There are some small communions who still break the bread by actually taking a loaf and breaking it, and there are some small communions who still use one silver cup from which they all drink. But with reference to the baptism of the Holy Spirit and the baptism by water in the Name of the Lord Jesus Christ when a believer is joining the church, there is no clear description in the Bible as to how it is done. The history of the church has produced two modes, each indicating that sins will be washed away by the blood of Christ.

The sacrament of baptism by the use of water in any mode has been used by Christians to advertise to the world that the person being baptized is openly confessing faith in Jesus Christ. The world has come to accept this practice of baptism as an accepted equivalent to public profession of faith in Jesus Christ. But this outward sign actually points to an inner reality when the believing soul receives the presence and the operation of the Holy Spirit. More is said in the New Testament about the baptism of the Holy Spirit, than about the baptism with water. John the Baptist himself taught plainly:

> I indeed baptize you with water unto repentance: but he that cometh after me is mightier than I, whose shoes I am not worthy to bear: he shall baptize you with the Holy Ghost, and with fire (Matthew 3:11).

From what Jesus of Nazareth taught about the working of the Holy Spirit we can understand why no sacrament has been instituted to symbolize the Baptism of the Holy Spirit.

> The wind bloweth where it listeth, and thou hearest the sound thereof, but canst not tell whence it cometh, and whither it goeth: so is every one that is born of the Spirit (John 3:8).

Yet this baptism of the Holy Spirit is actually the work of the living Lord Jesus Christ, and is essential to the life and experience of a Christian.

The baptism of the Holy Spirit results in certain specific gifts being found among believers.

> For to one is given by the Spirit the word of wisdom; to another the word of knowledge by the same Spirit; to another faith by the same Spirit; to another the gifts of healing by the same Spirit; to another the working of miracles; to another prophecy; to another discerning of spirits; to another divers kinds of tongues; to another the interpretation of tongues: but all these worketh that one and the selfsame Spirit, dividing to every man severally as he will (I Corinthians 12:8-11).

Some people seem to have paid more attention to these gifts than they have to the Holy Spirit Himself. The gifts were only outward indications that the Holy Spirit had been received. The one function of the Holy Spirit is that He will take the things of Christ and show them unto the believer. The Spirit Himself is invisible and what the Spirit does is to emphasize the truth about Jesus Christ. When the soul first becomes aware of the indwelling presence of God, the Scriptures use the language to say that he is "baptized with the Holy Ghost." The Holy Spirit is given only to believers in Christ. He takes the things of Christ and shows them to the believer. In this way God works in the soul, moving the believer to Him in and through the living Lord Jesus Christ.

> Now if any man have not the Spirit of Christ, he is none of his (Romans 8:9).

> For as many as are led by the Spirit of God, they are the sons of God (Romans 8:14).

> And grieve not the holy Spirit of God, whereby ye are sealed unto the day of redemption (Ephesians 4:30).

> Quench not the Spirit (I Thessalonians 5:19).

> But covet earnestly the best gifts: and yet show I unto you a more excellent way (I Corinthians 12:31).

> Wherefore, brethren, covet to prophesy, and forbid not to speak with tongues. Let all things be done decently and in order (I Corinthians 14:39-40).

27.

Use of Scripture in Receiving the Holy Spirit

Do you think anybody could receive the Holy Spirit at any time?

> Then said Jesus to them again, Peace be unto you: as my Father hath sent me, even so send I you. And when he had said this, he breathed on them, and saith unto them, Receive ye the Holy Ghost: whose soever sins ye remit, they are remitted unto them; and whose soever sins ye retain, they are retained (John 20:21-23).

These are the words by which the Lord Jesus Christ gave His disciples to understand that they were to receive from God a certain inward enablement. God Himself by His Holy Spirit was going to come into them and help them in their service.

One aspect of the gospel of the Lord Jesus Christ that is so wonderful is "Whosoever will may come." We rejoice in that. Anyone, any time can come to God, but not in any way. Believing souls must come God's way. Fortunately we have the Scriptures which teach us about this. Also, in the matter of receiving the Holy Spirit we have the record of the history of a group of persons who received the Holy Spirit: the disciples of Jesus of Nazareth. The disciples in themselves were a varied group. They ranged from fishermen to bankers. Yet they were a distinctive group. These disciples were believers in Christ Jesus. Not everybody was. This holds true today: not everybody is a believer. And it is only to the believer that the Holy Spirit can come.

When the Lord Jesus Christ was here, He called certain persons to be with Him that they might hear Him, receive Him and learn from Him. He was the living Incarnate Word of God and they were able to see Him, to handle Him and to be with Him. Today we have the written Word of God. We can read and study the Bible. We can be helped by the Holy Spirit to understand the Bible, just as those men were helped to follow and come to know Jesus of Nazareth. To receive the Holy Spirit as they did on the Day of Pentecost one must believe in God, in Jesus Christ, and in the Holy Spirit. One must believe that the Holy Spirit was existent in all eternity as one of the Godhead: God the Father, God the Son, God the Holy Spirit. If one does not believe in the Holy Spirit he is certainly not going to be able to receive Him.

If I do not believe in God, I could not expect God to save me. I must believe in the presence of the Holy Spirit. His presence is real. I must believe in His power, He is able. As God is able, as Christ is able, I must believe that the Holy Spirit is able also.

Jesus of Nazareth said with reference to the Holy Spirit, "whom the world cannot receive because it seeth Him not." If I am to be able to receive the Holy Spirit, I must "see" Him. As a matter of fact He is invisible to the physical eye; then in what sense could I see Him? The revelation about Him is written in the Scriptures so that I can understand Him. I must understand His being and understand His function. And if I did not understand Him, then I would not be able to receive Him, because that's exactly what the Lord said, "whom the world cannot receive because it seeth him not." It doesn't understand Him. "Neither knoweth him." When the word "know" is used in the New Testament it implies more than just know about. It means knowing Him for who He is, esteeming Him. Someone might say, "Do you know Tom Brown?" "Oh, I know who he is, but I don't know him." If I am to receive the Holy Spirit I must have some personal appreciation of God, of Jesus Christ, and of the Holy Spirit. The disciples had this because they had been personally prepared for the receiving of the Holy Spirit by the living Lord Jesus Christ.

Let me say again, if I am to receive the Holy Spirit of God, I must be prepared to receive Him. I must be converted, turned to God through Christ Jesus. Being converted means more than just turning to God, and being convinced about Jesus Christ. I must be convinced about His resurrection from the dead. Before the Day of Pentecost, the Lord Jesus showed His disciples that He was alive by the space of forty days while He was with them. Now think that over slowly. He was with them appearing and disappearing by the space of forty days during which time He showed them by many infallible proofs that He was actually literally raised from the dead. Then in full view of them all, He ascended into heaven. So if a person were prepared to receive the Holy Spirit as the disciples did, he must be convinced about the resurrection of Jesus Christ from the dead, that Jesus Christ is alive and that He is at the right hand of God because of His ascension.

Also such a person must be committed to do the will of God in witnessing. But the disciples were cautioned not to commence witnessing until they had received the promise of the Father(Acts 1:4).

To be personally prepared to receive the Holy Spirit, one must be converted to God, convinced about Jesus Christ in His resurrection, His ascension, His being in the presence of God, and committed to do the will of God. He must be corrected so far as his personal life is concerned and then receive the Holy Spirit as He comes to him.

To be sure those disciples had been three years with the Lord personally. You and I will not have that privilege, but we do have the written Word of the Old Testament and the New Testament, and by the help of His Holy Spirit as we read and study in the Bible, it will be for us as though we were with the Lord Jesus Himself personally. This will enable us to realize the truth of the coming of the Holy Spirit.

When I know He has been promised, and I know that God has sent Him, and I know that the Lord Jesus Christ has promised Him to me, then I can expect to have the presence of the Holy Spirit in my heart, "working in me to will and to do of His good pleasure" (Philippians 3:13).

28.

The Meaning of Walking in the Lord

Could you understand how a person could be walking in the Lord while following his daily routine of activity?

"And Enoch walked with God: and he was not; for God took him" (Genesis 5:24). I'm sure everyone who has ever read through Genesis is acquainted with this statement. There is scarcely anything else we know about this man Enoch, except this simple description of him: he walked with God and was not, for God took him.

The Bible deals with our problems in living, with the whole world, with God, and with ourselves as we live. In living there is always an element of the new, the unexpected. We may have old paths with which we are acquainted. Yet as far as life is concerned, each morning it's brand new. We have never lived through that day before. That's the way we live. It reminds us of Abraham of whom it says in the Bible, "he went out not knowing whither he went." That is more true of us than we realize. Often there are options. This calls for guidance. Or even better than guidance, this could call for a guide, someone to lead us along the way.

The important truth in the statement we are considering is "Enoch walked with God." That implies self-control. It is a matter of taking himself in hand and putting himself in this way, an intentional direction which immediately brings to our minds that a person does not casually walk with God. You do not just loaf along, drift along and find yourself walking with God. This was demonstrated when Jacob had his great vision, and was affected by that vision so much that he vowed a vow. The latter part of that vow was "I will surely give the tenth unto thee"; meaning from now on I'm going to serve God. This was deliberate intention. When it was said of Noah that "Noah walked with God," it was further stated: "Thus did Noah, according to all that God commanded him, so did he." This points to the idea of what it means to walk with God: "according to all that God commanded him."

Moses stated this idea even more clearly in speaking to the children of Israel just before they entered into the land of Canaan. In the history of Israel, for a period of some four hundred years, they were slaves in Egypt, but it was forty years from the time that they left Egypt until the time that they entered Canaan. The book of Deuteronomy records for us three major addresses that Moses made to the children of Israel in giving instruction as to how to live obediently to God.

> O that there were such a heart in them, that they would fear me, and keep all my commandments always, that it might be well with them, and with their children for ever! Go say to them, Get you into your tents again. But as for thee, stand thou here by me, and I will speak unto thee all the commandments, and the statutes, and the judgments, which thou shalt teach them, that they may do them in the land which I give them to possess it. Ye shall observe to do therefore as the Lord your God hath commanded you: ye shall not turn aside to the right hand or to the left. Ye shall walk in all the ways which the Lord your God hath commanded you, that ye may live, and that it may be well with you, and that ye may prolong your days in the land which ye shall possess (Deuteronomy 5:29-33).

This made it plain for them: "You shall walk in all the ways which the Lord your God commanded you." In presenting the history of Israel the Old Testament tells how God instructed Israel from time to time as to what they should do, and how Israel failed to do it.

In the gospel the New Testament promises something better.

> For what the law could not do, in that it was weak through the flesh, God sending his own Son in the likeness of sinful

flesh, and for sin, condemned sin in the flesh: that the righteousness of the law might be fulfilled in us, who walk not
after the flesh, but after the Spirit (Romans 8:3-4).

In other words God sent His Son into the world that we might be
saved, because you and I could never do it in ourselves. You and I
could never obey God as He should be obeyed, but God sent His Son
into the world to die for us, to make it possible for us to believe in
Him and to receive from Him His Holy Spirit who would incline us
into the will of God. We will then walk in the will of God because
the Spirit of His Son is in our hearts crying, "Abba, Father" and
moving us to act to please Him. Walking in the Lord means not
walking in our own wills. We will be walking in the Lord, by His
guidance, by His grace.

Paul writes, "I am crucified with Christ: nevertheless I live; yet
not I, but Christ liveth in me" (Galatians 2:20). By this he means to
say, "Not by my effort according to the law, but by the will of God
through Christ Jesus according to the grace of God given to me." I
live in liberty in Christ Jesus, and not according to regulations so
that I could qualify. The practical importance is seen in this word,
"Walk in the Spirit, and ye shall not fulfill the lust of the flesh"
(Galatians 5:16). Isaiah prophesied that the time would come when
the person who committed himself to God would be blessed in this
way: "And thine ears shall hear a word behind thee saying, This is
the way; walk ye in it." No longer need we try to remember
instructions. The indwelling Holy Spirit will guide us. He will guide
us from within as our Companion. The Christian may experience an
inward tension between the flesh, that he has in himself naturally,
and the Spirit, that is given to him of God. In the matter of walking
in the Lord we must decide, "Whose man am I?" The Lord Jesus
taught us plainly about this: "No man can serve two masters." It
cannot be self and Christ: either we will do as we please or we will
do as He pleases. Joshua stated it plainly when he said to the people,
"Choose ye this day whom ye will serve. As for me and my house we
will serve the Lord."

29.

The Practice of Walking in the Lord

Did you realize that when a Christian is walking in the Lord it is not so much a matter of where he is walking as it is how he is walking?

Our interest in this series of studies has been in learning about living as a Christian. What is actually involved in the life and experience of a person who is trusting in Jesus Christ? So often the idea seems to prevail that being a Christian is a matter of doing right, and acting in such a way that a person might resemble Jesus of Nazareth. Actually there is no doubt that Christ's way of living is righteous. This would be acceptable, even pleasing to God: "This is my beloved Son, in whom I am well pleased" (Matthew 3:17). And it is true that if a person is a believer in Christ, he will want to please God and to please Christ. As far as it goes this idea is sound and yet there is an aspect of it that needs to be noted here: no human being would ever be able to walk as Jesus of Nazareth walked. For Him, it required no effort to be pleasing to the Father. Paul himself testified, "And herein do I exercise myself, to have always a conscience void of offense toward God, and toward men" (Acts 24:16). This implies that real effort on the part of the believer is necessary. Paul also said, "I know that in me, that is in my flesh, dwelleth no good thing." And in the same context he said, "I am carnal, sold unto sin." All of this indicates the Christian is involved in a real problem with the flesh.

Walking in the Lord poses two problems: how shall I ever do it, and what will I be doing when I do it? In the first aspect, it is important to get started right. To live as a child of God I must be a member of His Body. This is not something that the natural man can achieve. It is not something in which a person exercises himself so

118

that he may pass some examination to qualify. This is a gift. I can rejoice to know this has been done for me. Being reconciled to God is the work of Jesus Christ our Lord. When I accept Him, I belong to Him.

> For by grace are ye saved through faith; and that not of yourselves: it is the gift of God: not of works, lest any man should boast (Ephesians 2:8-9).

This cannot be told too often. It is the wonderful truth of the gospel. I can be free if I receive Christ Jesus. I will be free when I receive Christ Jesus as my Savior and Lord, and not because of my own efforts, or my own strength, or by my own works. It is entirely by His grace that I have salvation. Thus I have eternal life, the unspeakable gift that comes from God.

The second phase of living and walking with the Lord is to stay in this relationship, to abide. Christ Jesus said, "Abide in me and I in you." Paul referred to this when he wrote "Christ in you the hope of glory." And again when Paul testified of himself, "I am crucified with Christ: nevertheless I live; yet not I, but Christ liveth in me" (Galatians 2:20). How will things go for me when I am living and walking with the Lord? This is made clear in Ephesians 4:1 "I therefore, the prisoner of the Lord, beseech you that ye walk worthy of the vocation wherewith ye are called." What does that actually mean? Notice what he goes on to say: "With all lowliness and meekness, with long-suffering, forbearing one another in love; endeavoring to keep the unity of the Spirit in the bond of peace." These are wonderful words, describing a way of life worthy of the Lord.

It is here we see what conduct will look like when I act in a way that is worthy of His Name. "With all lowliness": lowliness is the way I rate myself. "And meekness": that is how I react to injury from other people. In lowliness I point at me and consider others better than myself; in meekness I look at the other man and do not retaliate when he does wrong to me.

"With long-suffering": this will be needed. Any human being that is going to live with his fellow human beings in lowliness, letting others go first, taking the last place, will at times be abused. "And meekness": if I undertake to live with meekness and not retaliate there will be people who take advantage of me and if I continue doing this I will suffer; that will be "long-suffering." "With long-suffering, forbearing one another in love": forbearing one another means tolerating one another, enduring each other. "In love": because I seek their welfare. "Endeavoring to keep the unity of the Spirit in the bond of peace": not a matter of achieving unity but keeping the unity that is there. This emphasizes the fact that because the Holy Spirit is in the hearts of the believers they are actually in the Spirit as one, because there is just one Spirit.

And so when I talk about walking with the Lord, I am talking of walking with all lowliness and meekness, with long-suffering, forbearing one another in love, doing everything I possibly can to keep the unity of the Spirit in the bond of peace.

"This I say therefore, and testify in the Lord, that ye henceforth walk not as other Gentiles walk, in the vanity of their mind" (Ephesians 4:17). Don't walk the way the people of the world do in the vanity of their mind. Walking in the Lord will be in the light of God's Word. "That ye put off concerning the former conversation the old man, which is corrupt according to the deceitful lusts; and be renewed in the spirit of your mind; and that ye put on the new man, which after God is created in righteousness and true holiness" (Ephesians 4:22-24). What does it actually mean to say: "putting off the old man, putting on the new man?" Look at verse 25: "Putting away lying," which comes from the old man; "speak every man truth with his neighbor," which comes from the new man. Right here is a very simple formula. Do I have by any chance a disposition to color my story my way to make it sound good? Do I want to know how to quit that? Do I want to know how to overcome it? Then let me tell the truth! Because when I tell the truth, the plain fact is that I will not lie.

Notice how this works when I try not to hold grudges against people, so that I may forgive them now: " . . . let not the sun go down upon your wrath" (Ephesians 4:26). And in verse 28 note: "Let him that stole steal no more: but rather let him labor, working with his hands the thing which is good, that he may have to give to him that needeth." So the way for a Christian to stop stealing is to give to the poor! Ephesians 4:29-32 points the way to avoid saying nasty things in order not to grieve the Holy Spirit. Paul goes on to say that I should walk in love, as children of light (Ephesians 5:2-8). The Christian is to walk circumspectly: wisely, carefully. Finally in Ephesians 6:11 I am given some guidance as to how I can ever do this: "Put on the whole armor of God." We have been talking about the practice of walking in the Spirit, which means that Christ is walking in us. The Lord is working in me and in order to be walking in the Spirit I need to yield to let this happen in me by His grace and by His power.

30.

The Joy of Walking in the Lord

Do you understand how any person and especially any Christian person could have joy at all times?

"But the fruit of the Spirit is love, joy, peace . . . " (Galatians 5:22).

We've been thinking together about walking in the Lord; what it means to live dependent upon Him, and obedient to Him: walking in His presence, walking with Him. And now we read that "the fruit of the Spirit is love, joy, peace." We know what the Spirit will do. The Spirit will take the things of the Lord Jesus Christ and show them to us, and as we are made aware of what Christ Jesus has done for us, is now doing for us, and will do for us, our hearts are filled not only with love, but with joy. This enables us to understand the Apostle Paul when he says, "Rejoice in the Lord alway: and again I say, Rejoice" (Philippians 4:4).

When a person is urged to rejoice it is implied that this person already has joy. Only the person who has had something can regain it. So when we urge a person to "rejoice" we mean that he already has had "joy" in the Lord; now we want him to "rejoice, and again I say, Rejoice." It is a matter of urging a person who has had joy in the Lord to have this joy again. If I am a Christian because I believe in Jesus Christ, I belong to God and can call such things to my mind that will arouse joy in my heart. Paul said, "Rejoice in the Lord alway: and again I say, Rejoice." He wrote this because this is something you can do.

Joy and gladness are often coupled together, but they're not entirely alike. For example, I can be glad when things work out in a

122

certain way, but I can have joy if certain things are true regardless of what happens. One would not ordinarily speak of a person being glad in a time of sorrow, of being glad in a time of strain and stress, but one can have joy even in the dark hours of sorrow. One can have joy during dark events. I remember on one occasion when I was conducting a funeral service in a particularly pathetic situation. In this case a young wife died very suddenly while she was at work in her business office downtown. She had a brain hemorrhage and died. I was called in to conduct the funeral service. Her young husband had been out of town. He was so far away he didn't get in until the day of the funeral and when I went over to the funeral parlor to see him, my heart quailed within me. What could I ever say to this man? Here I was, alive and well, my wife was alive and well, my children were all living and well at that time. What in the world could I ever say to this person who had just lost his dear wife? And I remember the surprise I had when I got into the room and saw him. His face lit up when he saw me and he came over to shake my hand and his heart was bubbling over with joy. I could hardly understand it. He said to me, "Oh, isn't it wonderful? Isn't it wonderful?" I was expecting to find him broken, and shattered. Instead of that he was really rejoicing, and he looked at me rather closely. He said, "You understand, don't you?" I said, "I think I can, but tell me about it." I said, "What is it that gives you this joy?" "Oh," he said, "the Lord is here! The Lord is here! I don't have to go through this alone. Isn't that wonderful?" Well, it was wonderful, and it was a remarkable example of joy such as I hadn't seen in the very darkest hour. It's such a blessing to have this joy. The Bible says "the joy of the Lord shall be your strength."

Paul writes, "Rejoice in the Lord alway: and again I say, Rejoice. Let your moderation be known unto all men" (Philippians 4:4-5). This means your self-control, your consideration of other people, your yieldedness unto the will of God. "The Lord is at hand." The Lord will soon take a hand in things. So let this be known everywhere that all believers may rejoice. "Be careful for nothing," meaning, don't be worried, don't let yourself get overanxious; "but in everything by prayer and supplication with thanksgiving let your requests be made known unto God." You're going to have joy and this is the way to have it.

Ordinarily things that surround you and threaten you are the things that take away your joy. If you look at trouble, and you look at the things round about you that threaten you, you'll lose your joy. But if, instead of looking at them and letting them threaten you, you take them to God, you are no longer worried. You're not troubled about these things, "but in everything by prayer and supplication with thanksgiving let your requests be made known unto God. And the peace of God, which passeth all understanding, shall keep your hearts and minds through Christ Jesus" (Philippians 4:6-7).

> Finally, brethren, whatsoever things are true, whatsoever things are honest, whatsoever things are just, whatsoever things are pure, whatsoever things are lovely, whatsoever things are of good report; if there be any virtue, and if there be any praise, think on these things" (Philippians 4:8).

Taking that as a menu, looking over those statements and keeping those things in mind, I will find that joy will stay with me.

Paul has written of another instance of what makes us joyful: "By whom also we have access by faith into this grace wherein we stand, and rejoice in hope of the glory of God" (Romans 5:2). We can have joy in hope of the glory of God. What then is the glory of God? It is when God has His way, when He does what He wants to do within us. The confident expectation that "all things work together for good" will give us joy.

When you are living your life with a lot around you that troubles you, how can you have joy? First of all, let your moderation be known, your self-control: keep yourself under God. Remember the Lord is at hand. Confidently expect that whenever anything comes up that would worry you, with prayer and supplications with thanksgiving let your requests be made known unto God, and as in Romans, rejoice in hope of the glory of God. It's going to turn out

God's way and you'll have it the way God wants it. That's what the glory of God will be!

"We also joy in God through our Lord Jesus Christ" (Romans 5:11). How can we joy in God? By looking at His wisdom, His power, His grace, His benevolence, His kindness, by just thinking about God. God has everything in hand and He is on the throne. I do not need to worry. I can have joy to think that all is in God's hands. And the beauty of holiness will come to me to bless me. "These things have I spoken unto you, that my joy might remain in you, and that your joy might be full" (John 15:11). Previously in the first ten verses He said, "Abide in me and I in you." This fellowship with the Lord will actually help my joy to be full. Then again in verse 8 "that ye bear much fruit." Being fruitful makes for joy. When you consider that God is having His way in your life, that will make for joy. "Whatsoever ye shall ask of the Father in my name, he may give it you" (John 15:16).

If you were to put those things together: abiding in Christ and Christ abiding in you—you belonging to Him; letting God have His way in your life, and whatsoever you ask in His Name—He will give it to you! No wonder that John writes: "And these things write we unto you, that your joy may be full" (I John 1:4). John specifically mentions that these things that he is writing about, are about believing in Jesus Christ, about forgiveness and cleansing, about having an Advocate with the Father who will intercede for us, about loving the brethren, and getting answers to prayer. If I then as a Christian simply live conscious of His forgiveness, His cleansing, His love, I can tell you that deep down in my heart the springs of joy will be full and my heart will be filled with praise and thanksgiving to God. "The fruit of the Spirit is love, joy and peace."

31.

Warfare in Scripture

Do you think it would be possible for a man to live without fighting?

> From whence come wars and fightings among you? come they not hence, even of your lusts that war in your members? Ye lust, and have not: ye kill, and desire to have, and cannot obtain: ye fight and war, yet ye have not, because ye ask not. Ye ask, and receive not, because ye ask amiss, that ye may consume it upon your lusts. Ye adulterers and adulteresses, know ye not that the friendship of the world is enmity with God? whosoever therefore will be a friend of the world is the enemy of God (James 4:1-4).

In these straightforward and stern words James discusses the condition of mankind and points out that contention, strife, fighting and war are natural to man. Today there is a general outcry among us against war, as if war were a practice forced upon an unwilling and innocent people. You get the impression by hearing people talk that someone generated this idea of war and forced it upon the public when people really did not want it. Often the notion is expressed that we could have peace if warmongers would just leave us alone. But the contention that flares up into the open conflict that we call war is actually due to factors that are beyond our control. Let us look more closely at what James has written. "From whence come wars and fightings among you?" Where does conflict originate? "Come they not hence, even of your lusts that war in your members?"

The Apostle Paul writes about this:

> For the flesh lusteth against the Spirit, and the Spirit against

the flesh: and these are contrary the one to the other: so that
ye cannot do the things that ye would (Galatians 5:17).

And so the Bible reveals the fact there has always been opposition
and conflict in this world. Living in the natural world is never a nice,
peaceable, bland business. What it could have been without sin we
can only imagine. The only world that we know has sin in it. When
Adam took the forbidden fruit in the garden, when he reached for
the separated portion of which he had been told that he should not
eat thereof to please himself, sin entered into the world and with sin
came conflict. The first example of this conflict recorded in Scripture is when Cain killed his brother Abel. In the curse that followed
the sin of Adam, there is the intimation of continuous perpetual
contention and strife. The earth became a hostile environment. Now
thorns and thistles would grow.

Anybody seeking to have a garden knows about this. First there is
the soil itself. Have you ever prepared a garden? It is a back-tiring if
not a back-breaking job to do the digging, especially if you have to
do it by hand. Even if it is done mechanically, there is trouble in
preparing the soil. Then there is the weather. It cannot be controlled, yet it must be taken into mind. And there are the weeds.
Nothing has ever been cultivated to grow in a garden that didn't have
weeds. No one needs to plant them. They are there. Even after
something has been done about the weeds, there are the bugs. Also
there are diseases as well as marauders—dogs, cattle, chickens, birds.
As a matter of fact having a garden is not a simple operation.

If I should hear you say, "I don't believe we should fight. We
should just let nature take its course." What do you mean? No more
hoes in the garden? Just let the weeds grow? No more spraying? Just
let the bugs and diseases take over? No more antiseptics around the
hospital? Let the microbes and infection start? We're just going to
let things go? Would that be wise? Should there be no fighting at all?
Then we should not use any disinfectant? We should have no
quarantine? We should not restrict anybody even if smallpox is
around or spinal meningitis is around? We should have no isolation

wards at the hospital? Everybody should be free to go every place at any time? If men did not exercise constant vigilance in killing microbes, germs, organisms that would infect people the natural result would be death! Absolutely, men must fight if men are going to live.

In this same line of thought we should consider if we want any control. So far as our living in our community is concerned, do we want no police force? Do we want no jails? No penitentiaries? All of these things are our methods of defence against forces that hurt and that destroy. Where is a person going to stop?

At what point would you no longer resist evil? Sometimes it is implied that you could give up, you could give in, and you could yield rather than resist. But is this possible? Would you give in to disease? Would you give in to robbers and thieves? If you saw a child being abused by an older child, would you just say, "I don't think I should interfere." All this is implied in conflict and trouble. In this world in which we live the Bible will authorize us to be vigilant and diligent to protect that which is worthwhile.

32.

Warfare in Personal Experience

If a person accepted Christ and became a Christian, would that mean that he would now have no more trouble or conflict of any sort?

> Be sober, be vigilant; because your adversary the devil, as a roaring lion, walketh about, seeking whom he may devour: whom resist steadfast in the faith (I Peter 5:8-9).

Peter wrote this, stern as it is, for each of us. He wrote for anyone who is a Christian, man or woman, old or young. So much is being said about war, implying it is a wicked evil exercise. Actually war is inevitably evil inasmuch as men promote it and men are evil. The moment I say "war," you begin to think of man fighting against man, but that is not all there is about war. When war is waged men are seeking to save their lives and improve their circumstances. The Bible does say "Blessed are the peacemakers," but this is not, "Blessed are the peace talkers"; not, "Blessed are the peace lovers." This is, "Blessed are the peacemakers."

Peace, where there is no contention, no open conflict, is very desirable, but it is not natural. You will not find peace in the world waiting for you. Living is dangerous for every fish in the sea, every fowl in the air, every animal on the face of the earth, as well as every human being. Living is downright dangerous. Peace, when things under control are quiet and orderly, is an achievement. It is like health. Health is a wonderful blessing and it is natural to think that any living being would be healthy. Not so fast! A person is not necessarily born with health. Health is not automatic.

In this universe there are contrary forces. This can be seen even in such a natural event as walking. Any time a person stands up and walks there is a victory over the law of gravitation. The person is being pulled down to the earth at whatever his weight is. When a man weighs 150 pounds, the earth is pulling him down to the extent of 150 pounds. He must stand up against that pull. In the world there are things that are vital, which make for life; and there are things that are fatal, which make for death. There is food in the world, but there is also poison in the world. In the world among people there are friends, and there are foes.

Much has been said about pollution. Pollution is not really a new idea. We have had pure food laws for a long time. Food can be contaminated, can be polluted. Since the beginning of hygiene there has been quarantine procedure.

Living among people, the function of police to guide, regulate and protect is understood. Not only police but firemen also are engaged in activity that endangers their lives. In every city in every year some men are killed in the line of duty as firemen and as policemen. In every city there are building inspectors who examine buildings and condemn those that are unsafe in order to protect the people who live there. It would be very naive to hold the idea that if everything were natural all would be well.

We have not yet considered the additional peril of sin, of human perversity. This can be seen as one looks at a garden. Wherever there is a garden there is a situation that is under control. When God made the Garden of Eden and put man in it, He told the man "to dress it and to keep it." May I say then that if I want beans in my garden, I've got to dig, plow, hoe and spray them after they've grown, and I'm going to have to fence them to keep out the neighbor's cats and dogs. Anyone who has ever had a garden knows about war. The weapon of the garden is the hoe, and when a man uses a hoe in the garden and is hoeing those weeds he is at war. Farming is a sort of continuing warfare.

Now let us consider the classic promise in the Bible of a peaceful world. It is written that the time will come when men will beat their swords into plowshares and their spears into pruning hooks. Do you realize that a plowshare is something that will cut through the sod to turn over the earth, and the pruning hook is something that will cut off branches and trim trees? When swords are turned into plowshares and spears into pruning hooks, that will not be the end of fighting. It will be the end of fighting between people and animals. But it will certainly not be the end of fighting against elements, against weeds, or against dead, unfruitful branches.

The great human mistake is to blame other people for our trouble, as Cain did when he was having his own personal problem and projected that problem upon Abel. For this he killed him. But that act did not help Cain any; it only made things worse for him. By killing Abel Cain had not solved his own problem; he suffered unbearable judgment because of his own sin. Our warfare is with the forces of evil, not with people. We fight with the devil. Paul writes:

> For though we walk in the flesh, we do not war after the flesh: (for the weapons of our warfare are not carnal, but mighty through God to the pulling down of strongholds;) casting down imaginations, and every high thing that exalteth itself against the knowledge of God, and bringing into captivity every thought to the obedience of Christ (II Corinthians 10:3-5).

As surely as we live in this world we shall be involved in warfare with the flesh, with the powers of darkness and the forces of evil, but our victory is assured through Jesus Christ our Lord.

33.

War in Heaven

Can you realize that conflict and war occur in Heaven? The word Heaven is used in several different meanings in the Bible. The simplest meaning is to think of it as being where God is, as our Lord taught His disciples to pray, "Our Father, which art in Heaven." Also we use the word Heaven to refer to the spiritual world in contrast to this, the earthly world. It's common for us to think of Heaven as something way out there, far, far away. And there is a sense in which we can feel that way. But that is misleading: that is not true. Heaven is round about us. In the book of Job it is written Satan appeared in the presence of God among the sons of God, and that Satan argued with God. That was not on earth, that was in Heaven. Job, who lived on earth himself, never knew that what happened to him here on earth was actually inspired by the controversy between God and Satan in the heavenlies.

It would be idle to speculate as to why God created the devil, or why He tolerates him. It would be just as foolish for us to ignore what has been revealed about the devil in the Scriptures. The malicious activity of Satan, his vicious intention to destroy us, is much too serious a threat to be ignored so far as we are concerned. Peter warns us:

> Be sober, be vigilant; because your adversary the devil, as a roaring lion, walketh about, seeking whom he may devour: whom resist steadfast in the faith (I Peter 5:8-9).

Every word in that sentence is true. Living for us is a problem in this mixed-up world we are in; we are weak, ignorant, and sinful. All of this is compounded because there is an evil adversary, a sinister malicious enemy. Our Lord warned Peter:

> Simon, Simon, behold, Satan hath desired to have you, that he
> may sift you as wheat: but I have prayed for thee, that thy
> faith fail not: and when thou art converted, strengthen thy
> brethren (Luke 22:31-32).

Those words mean exactly what they say: "Satan [he's real], hath
desired to have you. [He can ask about you], that he may sift you as
wheat." He's got in mind to shake you up and show you up as being
worth nothing. That's his ambition, "but I have prayed for thee";
that's real. The Lord Jesus Christ in Heaven is actually praying for
His own.

So you're in trouble! So you're in your home! So you're in your
kitchen! So you're dealing with your children! So you're trying to
get along with your boss! "I have prayed for you." Round about
you there are evil things. You're in danger, "but I have prayed for
thee that thy faith fail not." The praying of the Lord Jesus Christ
wasn't a request that the devil drop dead. That's not what He prays
for; nor that all the things that are bad be changed to good. He prays
that your faith will not fail, because with faith in God you can go
through anything. "And when thou art converted, strengthen thy
brethren."

Perhaps so far as Christian people are concerned, there is no more
dangerous practice than to ignore the reality of Satan. Could you
imagine a hospital that would ignore the danger of infection? Can
you think of an operating room with doctors performing surgical
operations that would pay no attention to the danger of infection?

The whole serious truth is more vividly revealed to us in a
remarkable passage in Revelation 12:7:

> And there was war in heaven: Michael and his angels fought
> against the dragon; and the dragon fought and his angels, and
> prevailed not; neither was their place found any more in
> heaven.

There was war in Heaven! Let us beware that we do not think of
Heaven being away, way off, millions of miles away. Heaven is all

around us. It's the invisible world, the spiritual world. God is everywhere; Heaven is everywhere. This isn't the phase of Heaven that you and I will rest in. Eventually we will be in the presence of God when Satan has been put away. But just now, where the Spirit of God is, there is Heaven. Living in this world we are in the midst of a battlefield. We are very much involved because the issue at stake in this war that is going around us is our souls.

Paul was very conscious of this struggle. Paul writes in II Corinthians 10:3-4:

> For though we walk in the flesh, we do not war after the flesh: (for the weapons of our warfare are not carnal, but mighty through God to the pulling down of strongholds).

And again in Ephesians 6:11-17: "Put on the whole armor of God, that ye may be able to stand against the wiles of the devil." The devil is real and so is his attempt to trick you. If he could lead you into doing something selfish or self-indulgent, he would win. He wants to get the believer out of the will of God, as it is written:

> For we wrestle not against flesh and blood, but against principalities, against powers, against the rulers of the darkness of this world, against spiritual wickedness in high places (Ephesians 6:12).

This is true right here round about us.

> Wherefore take unto you the whole armor of God, that ye may be able to withstand in the evil day, and having done all, to stand. Stand therefore, having your loins girt about with truth (Ephesians 6:13-14).

This is just not any kind of truth. This is truth about God, truth about Jesus Christ.

"Having your loins girt about with truth, and having on the breastplate of righteousness." And what that means is careful believing obedience. Christians are to make it a point to do what God wants them to do in a way that will be right in His sight.

"And your feet shod with the preparation of the gospel of peace." Believers are to be conscious of the victory of Jesus Christ: that is the gospel of peace. We need to have in mind all the time, Christ Jesus is the victor!!

"Above all, taking the shield of faith, wherewith ye shall be able to quench all the fiery darts of the wicked." In every situation the believer should remember God and His promises. Using the shield of faith, no matter what comes up, the Christian can lift up his eyes unto God: he can believe in Him. "Satan trembles when he sees, the weakest saint upon his knees." That is the hope of the believer.

"And take the helmet of salvation." Believers are to think of what God is doing: this is the helmet of salvation. "And the sword of the Spirit, which is the word of God." Of all that armor described in this passage, the only item that is to be used for offense is the sword of the Spirit: the Word of God! The equipment in the armor of God is spiritual, internal and personal.

The real issue in this war, as in all conflicts for a Christian, is actually human nature. James asks, "Whence comes wars and fightings among you?" and then points out it is from within. The key to my victory is lodged in my self-control, so that I should seek to be able to say like Paul, "I keep under my body that I might obey him."

We are to think about Christ Jesus because the victory belongs to Him. Power belongeth to God. "All power is given unto me," said the Lord Jesus Christ. It is written in the Scriptures, "He is able to save to the uttermost those that come unto God by him." Yes, there is war in Heaven, but through our great Lord and Savior, the Captain of our salvation, there is victory in Christ Jesus.

34.

Blessed Are They That Hunger

Did you know that the power of God is received by those who humbly ask for it in faith?

Do I need to do anything to be blessed of God? Some say that the believer doesn't need to do anything. God does it all. But, is this so? Consider even in such a simple thing as your garden. It is true that in Eden the garden was prepared and Adam was put into it by the Providence of God; but he was told to dress it and to keep it. It is true that God makes the beans grow, but man cultivates the garden, and man plants the beans and waters the beans. It is written: "I have planted, Apollos watered; but God gave the increase" (I Corinthians 3:6). This is emphasized by a certain aspect of the law of the harvest: "Whatsoever a man soweth that shall he also reap." In fact, Paul writes this, "He which soweth sparingly shall reap also sparingly, and he which soweth bountifully shall reap also bountifully" (II Corinthians 9:6). We are noting there is a direct relation between what we do and what we receive, and such is the testimony of believing people in the Bible.

Of all those whom we read about in the Bible, who sought the face of the Lord for help, Jacob is perhaps the classic example. When he, with his families and his flocks and herds, was returning after having worked for his uncle Laban for twenty years, he heard that Esau was coming to meet him with four hundred men (Genesis 32:24-28). When Jacob knew that Esau was coming to meet him, he was afraid. Esau had threatened to kill Jacob twenty years before. When Jacob realized he had to meet Esau the next day he went to God in prayer. That night he was alone with God. He wrestled with a messenger sent from God that he might be blessed and that wrestling went on all night long. Before it was finished Jacob was crippled. His thigh was broken, but he would not let go. He received a new name because he persisted in clinging to his messenger until he received the blessing of God. In all Scripture this is the outstanding demonstration of how a man receives the blessing of God.

In meeting Esau, Jacob was meeting the consequences of his own past conduct. It was what he had done when he and his mother had deceived his father, Isaac, and had received the blessing which ordinarily would have gone to Esau, that angered his brother when he heard about it. Isaac the father had been tricked into thinking he was giving the blessing to Esau. Hearing of this deception Esau vowed that he would kill Jacob. Now twenty years later, Jacob is meeting this threat!! This rings a solemn note in our own hearts.

Each of us has a past. Somewhere in the course of our living there are not only wrong things we have done, but there are right things we haven't done. In God's plan there comes a time when the soul comes face to face with the consequences of its own past.

Jacob was also aware that he was personally unable to cope with the situation. He knew he couldn't do it, but at the same time he believed that God could. There is no mention here as to what kind of man Jacob was, because God does not look at him to evaluate him in comparison with other people. The truth is that Jacob believed God could and he believed God would, because of former experiences that he had had with God. So he persisted. He persevered in praying until the answer came.

There are more instances of others who received blessing. Hannah was one of two wives, and she had a personal problem. The other woman was preferred before her because the other woman had children, and Hannah had none. This gave Hannah great distress, and in that situation Hannah was personally helpless. There wasn't a thing she could do about it. But she believed in God, and believed God could change matters. She prayed earnestly and her prayer was granted. She became the mother of Samuel.

Naaman the Syrian was a great military man, but he was a leper.

Leprosy was a disease that in those days was considered incurable, so that Naaman as a leper was really helpless. He was told by a captive Jewish maid that there was a prophet in Israel who could bring the power of God to bear upon him. Naaman came over to find Elisha and to ask him for help. Eventually Elisha instructed him, telling him to go down to the River Jordan and bathe seven times. At first Naaman was dissatisfied with that, and would not do it, but he humbled himself and meekly obeyed and was cleansed.

Daniel was another example. When Daniel knew that there had been an order that no one was to worship anybody or anything except as the Emperor authorized, Daniel was unaffected by the king's command. He opened his window and three times a day he prayed to his God, the God of Jerusalem. This resulted in Daniel being thrown into the lion's den. But God delivered him there.

The New Testament likewise has examples of people receiving the blessing of God. There is the touching case of the leper. How simple it was! The leper came to Jesus of Nazareth, "Lord, if thou wilt, thou canst make me clean." Jesus of Nazareth looked on him with compassion: "I will, be thou clean." And immediately his leprosy was cleansed! For me that is just marvelous!

Consider the centurion, who was coming on behalf of his servant. When he came to Jesus of Nazareth he said, "Lord, speak the word only and my servant will get well." Jesus of Nazareth was amazed and said, "I have not found faith like that, not in all Israel." He did speak the word and the servant did get well. Consider again the woman with the issue of blood, who was saying in her heart, "If I could just touch the hem of His garment" as she pushed through the crowd, and reaching through touched the hem of His garment, immediately the flow of blood was stopped. She was healed.

Perhaps the classic example in the New Testament of those who really were blessed in their faith in the Lord is Mary of Bethany. She brought the precious box of ointment and anointed Jesus of Nazareth. When this incident occurred and she was criticized for spending so much money for this precious box of ointment, Jesus of Nazareth said, "Leave her alone. She hath done what she could." That story is very beautiful, but back of that story there was another incident. In Luke 10:38-42 it is written Martha was cumbered with much serving. She came to Jesus of Nazareth saying, "Lord, dost thou not care that my sister hath left me to serve alone? Bid her therfore that she help me." Jesus turned to her, "Martha, Martha, thou art careful and troubled about many things. . . . Mary hath chosen that good part, which shall not be taken away from her." This reveals the whole truth as to why Mary did as she did. Mary gave the very best that she had as a gift to the Lord because she was the one who sat at His feet and heard His words. She understood and believed in Him.

Blessing from God comes to the believer in response to his seeking it. Would I like to have more help? Then I should draw nigh to God about it. I should read my Bible and pray about it. It is absolutely true that "he that soweth sparingly, shall reap sparingly." If I do not ask I will not receive. But he that soweth bountifully shall also reap bountifully. This is also absolutely true, with reference to the blessing of God: if I ask for it, I will get it. If I ask for more, I will get more. "Ask and you shall receive. Seek and you shall find. Knock and it shall be opened unto you." These are the gracious promises of our living Lord and Savior, Jesus Christ.

35.

The Quest for Spiritual Power in Scripture

Do you realize that to have hunger is a sign of good health?

> Blessed are they which do hunger and thirst after righteousness: for they shall be filled (Matthew 5:6).

This is one of the Beatitudes. It is important to recognize that hunger as such is not bad. In fact it is a good sign of good health, but hunger as such is never good enough. Hunger in itself is a feeling of uneasiness. It is because we are not satisfied, because there is something else that we feel we need or want, that we could have. Probably one of the first reactions that an infant has is the desire for food. Actually the baby also needs to sleep, but it doesn't know that, whereas it seems to be aware of the need of food. It wants food because drinking feels good and eating feels good. A baby will turn away from food any time if it can get anything else that promises to give it more pleasure. Every person who has tried to feed a child will know this.

Generally, we say that we hunger for anything when we want it very much. If I have a longing desire for something, I will say, "I'm just hungry for that." Thus we have the expression: "I'm just hungry for a sight of such and such a person." Being hungry for something gives it top priority. "Blessed are they which do hunger and thirst after righteousness." The important word in that sentence is the last word, "righteousness." When we say "hunger and thirst after righteousness" we mean there is a certain result that we want that comes from being right with God. We could say, "Blessed are they which do hunger and thirst to be right with God." There is such a thing as having the desire in heart and mind that you really want to be right with God; you want to be well-pleasing: you yearn to be right with God.

But how could a sinner ever be righteous? Because you and I, as we read these words, know very well there is none righteous, no not one. We know that there is no man that sinneth not. We know that all have sinned and come short of the glory of God. Then what can we do about this? "Blessed are they which hunger and thirst after righteousness." The rest of that sentence is "for they shall be filled." Really? Well let me ask you this, Can a leper ever be clean? When I remind you of Naaman the Syrian and you'll say, "Oh, yes. He can be cleansed." Can a blind man see? Then you will think of Bartimaeus. "Oh, yes, the blind can see when their eyes are opened." Can a dishonest man ever be honest? Then you may think of Zaccheus. Oh, yes! If a man has been touched with the presence of the Lord and has been with Jesus of Nazareth, he can actually get to the place where he will restore anything he has taken unlawfully, and even give half his goods to feed the poor. That is what Zaccheus did. Can a dead man ever live? And then you will think of Lazarus. Oh, yes, a dead man can live, for God can raise the dead. Can an unreliable man ever be true? And you could think about Peter. "Men have called you Simon but you shall be called Peter." Men have called you a name that means "like sand" but they're going to call you a name that means "like rock." Can a prejudiced person, a person that's absolutely against the gospel, against the Lord, and against the Bible, can such a prejudiced person ever become a real believer? And then you must think about Paul. Oh, yes! That is possible. It has happened. So we can say "Blessed are they which do hunger and thirst after righteousness: for they shall be filled."

The individual is a sinner: there is no man that sinneth not. Can the sinner actually become righteous? Can a sinner ever really and truly be clean? By itself the word "clean" could be misleading, because when you say "clean" you are inclined to think that person has never done anything wrong. But you and I are not like that. It is better to use the word "cleansed." Can a leper ever be clean? Yes, because the leprosy can be cleansed. Can a sinner ever be clean? Yes, because the blood of the Lord Jesus Christ will cleanse us from all sin. It is written in the Beatitudes, "Blessed are the pure in heart for they shall see God." You may ask yourself, "Is there anybody ever pure?" If instead of the word "pure" we used the word "purified," counting on the cleansing by the blood of the Lord Jesus Christ, we would have the truth. One of the most wonderful things about our salvation by the Lord Jesus Christ is not only that He puts His hands as it were under your armpits and lifts you up, but He will not let you go. "Blessed are they which do hunger and thirst after righteousness." Oh, how wonderful! "They shall be filled." You can have it.

Sometimes this hunger is felt in despair. There may be some who feel "I'm just no good." Take heart, brother. If you come from the bottom of your heart and soul to say, "I'm just no good," I can assure you right now you could rejoice. You would be more than half-way home! Because the first thing you must get clear in your mind is that you are not personally worth anything. Repentance comes easier to a man that doesn't amount to anything. If you once know that you're not worth anything, you can let go of yourself and let God come in. Take heart, brother! You can have courage now, sister! There's something ahead for you. You're more than half-way home!

Sometimes this hunger takes the form and shape of shame. A person has the feeling, "I'm just not any good and what's worse I have never been any good," so that deep down in his heart he feels shame. That's a good sign! That shows that he knows better, and it shows that he wants better.

Sometimes this hunger appears in a discontent. When you're discontented with yourself it is easy to be discontent with everybody, irritable, critical of other people, uncomfortable all the way around in every way. This is not pleasant to experience but actually this also can be good. I am not saying this just to make you feel good. Actually I do want to encourage you to come to the Lord. If you wait to fix yourself up, you will never make it. Come as you are to the Lord Jesus Christ, and He will fix you up. And you will be acceptable to God in Christ Jesus. Do you want to be well-pleasing in the sight of God? Are you tempted to think, "When I get certain habits under control and I quit certain things, then I will be?" It will never happen that way. Come to the Lord as you are and trust in Him. Put yourself in his hands.

Would you want to be what you could be and what you should be? Then turn everything over to the Lord. Are you troubled because at times you don't even want this as much as you should? At times you may have the feeling in your heart, "I don't even care about it." That would be all the more reason to "Come to the Savior, make no delay." You can come to Him and be assured that He will be with you and for you. You can be certain that He wants to give you what you need for your peace and for His Glory.

36.

The Quest for Spiritual Power
in the Church

Do you realize that earnest souls in the history of the gospel among Christians in the church on earth have always been eager to achieve, to gain spiritual power?

"But what things were gain to me, those I counted loss for Christ" (Philippians 3:7). The Apostle Paul was a Jew, a Pharisee, and very zealous in his faith. When he became a Christian he said:

> But what things were gain to me, those I counted loss for Christ. Yea doubtless, and I count all things but loss for the excellency of the knowledge of Christ Jesus my Lord: for whom I have suffered the loss of all things, and do count them but dung, that I may win Christ, and be found in him, not having mine own righteousness, which is of the law, but that which is through the faith of Christ, the righteousness which is of God by faith: that I may know him, and the power of his resurrection, and the fellowship of his sufferings, being made conformable unto his death; if by any means I might attain unto the resurrection of the dead (Philippians 3:7-11).

Thus he described the prevailing purpose of his heart. He wanted to know more of Christ and be stronger in Him. Gaining spiritual power has always been the ambition of any intelligent sincere believer.

After all, if God has given to us Christ Jesus and in Him we have all things, we certainly should not live down here at this poor dying rate. We should be able to have help, even as we need help. Paul spared nothing in this quest. He emptied himself of self, not only of the things that were bad, but even of the things that were good, even of the things in which he could have been proud. He emptied them all out as if they were nothing, and threw them away as if they were refuse, that he might win Christ. Paul makes it clear that if we bring in the Lord Jesus Christ everything else must go out. He himself put everything else out first, that Christ might come in. He understood the problem, as the problem of his flesh. "But I keep under my body, and bring it into subjection: lest that by any means, when I have preached to others, I myself should be a castaway" (I Corinthians 9:27). Christians can do this. We can achieve spiritual power by obeying the Living Lord. We should heed the words of Peter, "Abstain from fleshly lusts, which war against the soul" (I Peter 2:11).

Since fleshly desires prevailed in the world among people, the idea took hold among the early Christians that the real way to win for the true earnest Christian would be to withdraw from the world. We can be rather amused when we read of one of the early Christians by the name of Simon. He felt that the sinfulness of people stimulated his own sinfulness. In order to get away from people he climbed to the top of a high column and stayed there. The column was called a style; we don't use that word today but it actually means a high post, a column. This man would climb to the top of that column, and for this he was given the nickname "Simon the Stylite." Later on, there developed among Christian people a tendency to withdraw in this fashion. As a result there came to be a number of hermits. These withdrew themselves so that they would be away from the tempting things of the world and the sinful suggestions of other people. But the hermit had one problem that was not recognized at that time. "It's not good for a man to be alone." Not even in a good cause, it is not good for him to be alone.

Later there were those who gathered together in groups. They withdrew from the public, and from the world, but they lived together as brothers in a monastery, and were spoken of as monks. They really tried to help each other to become sincere believers. They made themselves strict rules which they followed. They had careful regulations. It was characteristic of them that no man could own anything. Each had to turn everything over to the group while he lived there and worked there. He performed his service and worshipped God, seeking to stay away from the world, in the sincere desire to be true in spirit and to witness to the Lord. In time because they really wanted to do the will of God and were just as sincere as I can make the word sound to you, it came to them as from the Spirit of God, that they should do things for other people. So they began a personal aid plan and while they lived to themselves, withdrawn from everybody else, the monastery became a sort of a haven of refuge. Anybody in trouble could come there. It became a hospital, and the sick could come to the monastery and the monks would take care of them. It was a refuge for the person who was in flight from anywhere, and anyone that came in there was safe as long as he was in the monastery. It was a school, the ignorant would come there to be taught by the monks and then afterwards the nuns would busy themselves in helping other people. There were some great names added to the history of the church at that time.

One of the most famous was Saint Francis of Assissi; and anyone familiar with the story will know that Saint Francis as a young man was a rich nobleman, very worldly, given over to all kinds of ungodly practices. Then with all his wealth and learning, with all his sin, this man turned to the Lord Jesus Christ and became a most earnest believer. He had lived a fastidious life, taking care that he didn't dirty his hands with anything unclean. When he entered the monastery to become a monk, he was assigned to work in the hospital. There he requested that he be given the most menial tasks that he might discipline his flesh. This was done. He started his work in the hospital, scrubbing floors and carrying out bed pans. In this way he aimed to humble himself. He became famous as a Christian. Another famous believer was a man named Thomas á Kempis. He wrote a splendid devotional book, which we still read, "The Imitation of Christ." Thomas á Kempis studied and searched his own heart to find out how to grow as a Christian. He found out that the thing to do was to be like the Lord Jesus Christ. Actually as Christians, you and I cannot be in ourselves like Christ, but we can let Christ be in us.

The monks and nuns in the monasteries were godly, sincere people, always with the same intention to honor God. They did everything they could think of to gain spiritual power. In order to help themselves grow in devotion they took vows of chastity, poverty, and charity. They held themselves strictly under control. Yet they were not wholly successful in their aim. They were human beings despite all their efforts. Even though these dedicated people did have such faith in God, in time the monasteries became corrupt. Some became wealthy. Their leaders became covetous. The monks and nuns worked for no pay and in time some monasteries simply became rich. Soon it followed, they had sin even among themselves. This demonstrated the fact that the one thing that the hermits, monks, and nuns had in common was their human nature. Withdrawing from the world was impossible because the world was in them.

There were other attempts to achieve piety in the history of the church. When the monks realized that being withdrawn was causing them to become covetous and selfish and proud, some of them tried a different procedure and became friars. These took the same vows as the monks but they didn't live in a monastery. They went out among the people doing good. They became an order of traveling priests, helping wherever needed among the people.

This brief review has been based on history and will serve to show that this problem of growing in grace in the Lord Jesus Christ has always been the ambition and the goal of sincere Christians. The person who believes in the Lord Jesus Christ and appreciates the fact that he has been saved, wants to glorify Him, wants to do something for Him. The persons we have noted demonstrated that this goal could not be reached in themselves. It would be in the way they yielded themselves to God. In the history we noted the Christians tried yielding themselves to God by withdrawing from people and the world. They needed to learn as we know today that the only way in which we can be free from the world, the only way in which we can be free from the sinful influences is by yielding ourselves in our own hearts to the living God. Christians must turn to Him.

In the midst of everything I must walk alone with Him, even as the three Hebrew children walked with Him in the fiery furnace back in the book of Daniel. He is my God and my Savior and when I want His blessing in me I must seek His face as I yield to the Holy Spirit He has given to me in my own heart.

37.

Elements in Promoting Spiritual Experience

Do you know there are certain steps a person can take that will result in having faith, and in growing stronger in faith?

What would be the result in any person who would truly receive Christ, become a Christian? No doubt many who read these lines are already committed to the Lord Jesus Christ and are rejoicing in their faith in Him. They are trusting Him. I hope there will be some reading these pages who have heard about Jesus Christ. Some of these may even be hoping some day to yield to Him. They may intend some time to turn to Him, perhaps something is holding them back for the time being. There may always be a few who feel deep down in their hearts that there's nothing to the gospel, that what we are saying is just our idea and not real. To all of these I want to point out there are steps which, if taken, will result in growing faith within that person. We know that as soon as a person receives Christ Jesus he is adopted as a child of God. The believer is immediately treated by the Father according to the promises in the gospel. It is true that a believer can be blessed with a growing faith. His faith can become stronger, his assurance can be real.

As a believer, I can draw actually nearer to God. Faith is more than an attitude or a willingness. It has a content: I actually believe something. It is not only true that I believe as such, but what I believe about the Lord Jesus Christ can actually be set forth. Faith that saves the soul is taking God's promise which is set forth in the Scripture and which was demonstrated incarnate in Jesus of Nazareth, and holding it, clinging to it as real. The promise of God is "whosoever believeth in Him shall never perish but have everlasting life." How can I ever have such faith?

The first step toward saving faith is to read the Bible. Faith is based on the Bible. I must trust it. The Lord Himself said:

> The wind bloweth where it listeth, and thou hearest the sound thereof, but canst not tell whence it cometh, and whither it goeth: so is every one that is born of the Spirit (John 3:8).

There is no doubt of the outcome if I will read the Bible and listen to it. "Blessed is he that readeth, and they that hear the words of this prophecy, and keep those things which are written therein" (Revelation 1:3). If I want faith in Christ, I must read the Bible. If I want *more* faith in Christ, I must read the Bible more. If I have any doubts or questions, I should read the Bible for my answers. I must keep on reading it and studying it. The more I read the Bible the stronger my faith will be.

The second step to faith is also very well known, even if it isn't practiced much: the second step is praying. On the basis of what I read in the Bible, the promises that I hear there, I can be praying to Almighty God. In that praying I will praise Him, I will thank Him, I will bring my own needs, my petitions before Him. I will ask for blessing. I will pray daily. It may be that I have some special time for prayer such as praying in the morning or praying in the evening; and I may pray privately. Also I will pray as a routine at mealtime. Each time I sit down to a meal, I give thanks. And I will pray with my family, even as I will pray in private. You might not think this is important because you may not think you are important, but whoever you are such praying will matter.

There is a real advantage in cultivating praying if I have a fixed time to pray. If I make it a point that I am going to pray in the morning before I go to work, it will be easy enough to remember that before I start work I pray. If I have in mind I am going to pray at night before I go to bed, because I have made this a regular habit in my life, then when I go to bed, it will occur to me that this is the time when I will pray to God. All this is helpful, because of the kind of people we are: we get so involved and so mixed up we just don't find time for the things that we really want to do.

In the same way, it is helpful to have a settled place for prayer. For instance if I make it a point to pray at my bedside, it is gratifying that often just going to the bedside and kneeling there will bring me into a mood and attitude of prayer. It may be that you pray sitting in a certain chair. Wherever that may be make it a fixed place: go there to pray. Sometimes it helps to have a prayer list. There will be certain things for which I want to pray. I may have them in mind and keep them in my memory. But it would not do any harm to make a list of the things I want to pray for and keep it before me. You might ask me what should be put on the list; and I would tell you, put on it anything that bothers you. Just anything! Whatever it is that you're concerned about. Tell God where it hurts. There can be no doubt that praying will warm your soul.

The third step that I can take to cultivate my faith is to worship. That means more than just going to church. It will include going to church, but it is more than that. And it is more than just a frame of mind. Worship is something I do, and there are good helps that will promote worship at once. Honor the Sabbath Day. "Remember the Sabbath Day to keep it holy." Just simply think of the Lord's Day as different. Treat Sunday differently from any other day. Another help for me will be to give some of my money. I could tithe my money, but if I am not ready to give the tenth of my income, I could make sure I give something to the Lord's work. I know that worship is an attitude of heart, but there are steps I can take that will help my attitude of heart. Another step I can take is service for God. I can commit myself to do something for Him. This may be related to the church program. In the church service, I can priase Him, I can give thanks to Him, and I may try to do His will. I can take part in service toward my fellowman: to those that are over me, I will show respect, to those who are equal to me, I will be considerate and to those who are poorer than I am, I will exercise charity. Always in dealing with people and with God, I will be acting in obedience to the will of God, seeking His approval. When each day is over, I will ask myself, Did I do anything today for the Lord's sake? And if I can't think of anything, I can start right then and praise God. Just thank Him for something. That will be a beginning.

A final step will be witnessing. I mean to let other people know that I believe. At home, or in the office, let them know that I believe. I have great sympathy for people who cannot talk about their faith. When I first became a Christian I found it hard to talk to strangers about my faith in God. But I found out a way to do it: a way that is easy and effective. Just carry a Bible! Have a pocket Testament or a small Bible and let it be seen that I have it! You would be surprised how that will witness. "Whosoever confesseth me before men, him will I confess before my Father, which is in heaven." Just as surely as you will take these steps I can promise you will grow in grace and in knowledge. Keep practicing them and walk with Him, and you will be blessed with more and more faith.

38.

Use of Scripture in Promoting Spiritual Experience

Can you see how fortunate a Christian is that the strength and growth of his faith and of his spiritual experience is directly related to Bible reading?

"If you abide in me and my words abide in you, you shall ask what you will and it shall be done unto you." These are the words of Jesus of Nazareth, speaking to His disciples, telling them that in the days to come when His personal presence, His physical body, would be taken away and He would have sent His Holy Spirit to be in them, and with them, if then they would abide in Him, and let Him abide in them, they would have constant blessing. We are interested in what happens in a Christian when he is fully given over to the Lord. When that is done so far as the Christian is concerned, his spiritual life, his personal faith, is directly involved in his Bible reading. "If you abide in me and my words abide in you, you shall ask what you will and it shall be done unto you."

Spiritual life and strength is very similar in operation to physical life and strength. If you think about living as a human being, you know you need food and you know you must have exercise: these things are essential. It is just that way in spiritual living. While spiritual things are invisible and intangible so that you cannot handle them and you cannot see them, the Christian is fortunate in that what he can do to promote his spiritual experience has been revealed to him. This is the consequence of the incarnation of the Word of God in the person of Jesus Christ. And what is it that we can do spiritually that will cause us to live and grow in the Lord? We can read the Bible. "Faith cometh by hearing and hearing by the Word of God." The Bible is the means for promoting spiritual experience.

God has spoken in the Scriptures for our learning. "All scripture is given by inspiration of God, and is profitable for doctrine, for reproof, for correction, for instruction in righteousness: that the man of God may be perfect, thoroughly furnished unto all good works" (II Timothy 3:16-17). The Scriptures were written that Christians by reading and studying them might be strong and fruitful. "For whatsoever things were written aforetime were written for our learning, that we through patience and comfort of the scriptures might have hope" (Romans 15:4). And so the Bible was written for that very purpose. Christians should read it and trust it! God will come to the believing heart. Paul was referring to things that were reported in the Old Testament when he wrote: "Now all these things happened unto them for examples: and they are written for our admonition, upon whom the ends of the world are come" (I Corinthians 10:11).

Reading the Scriptures is like living. There is much to be experienced. In reading the Bible the believer finds history, i.e., the history of the children of Israel, and as he reads about their experiences he will get the general idea of how God deals with His people. The reader will also find biography, the life of individual persons such as Abraham, Isaac, Jacob, Joseph, Moses, Hannah, David, Mary of Bethany and many others.

For me personally, as I read I come to know these different individuals and learn lessons that apply to my own personal life. Also I will find poetry: the book of Job, then the books of the Psalms, Proverbs, Ecclesiastes and the Song of Solomon. If I wanted to become a praying person, I would be hindered because I would not know what to say. I would not know how to say it. But I could take some of the Psalms, even the shorter Psalms, and learn by reading them. The language is language that will express the thoughts of the Spirit, and so as I read that language of the poetical Scriptures I learn the vocabulary, the words that I would use for the expression of devotion. The poetical books are very useful because I can read them for the expression of my own soul's thought in worship. I can actually worship God as I read the Psalms.

There is a portion of the Old Testament that is called the Prophets, which can be read to learn the thoughts of God about His people. For example in reading Isaiah it is not necessary to remember from beginning to end, all at one time. I can read verse by verse, and as I read it through I will see how often the light will shine into my soul and will actually show me the mind and the will of God about His people. In the New Testament are found the Gospels, which present manifestation of the truth of God. As I read Matthew, Mark, Luke, and John any day of the week, at any hour of the day I read about Jesus of Nazareth and see the Word of God incarnate. There I can see exactly who God is, and how God does, and what God says, plainly a demonstration of the truth of God. This is very helpful to a Christian. After the Gospels the reader comes to the book of the Acts of the Apostles, and there is revealed the example of the early believers. If I want to know what it means to be a Christian, I only need to read in the book of Acts. If I believe in the Lord Jesus Christ, what I read in the book of Acts is mine. That could happen to me. After the book of Acts the reader comes to the Epistles written by the apostles to the early Christians which will give an understanding of what it means to believe in the Lord Jesus Christ.

In reading the Bible, I will find stories, narratives. I need to know them to tell them to my children. They sketch the course of affairs under God. I can read what happened to Abraham, Moses, Joshua, David, Hezekiah, and many others. When I read those stories I will learn what happens under the hand of God. The Bible also has in it certain types. For example when I read about the Tabernacle, the place of worship in the Old Testament, I am learning how to worship God. When I read about the sacrifices and the Lamb of God, I am actually seeing a picture of the Lord Jesus Christ. When I read about the children of Israel being brought out of Egypt I can see how I am being brought out of the natural world. The types in Scripture actually will structure ideas of the truth. As I read them, I get ideas of the concepts of faith: they become diagrams that I can use to see the whole truth.

Also the Bible contains promises which will guide by challenging response. "Call upon me and I will answer thee." "Ask and you shall receive." Then again there are parables which illustrate. They are not hard to read, but they help me to learn profound truths. This can be felt when I read the parable of the Sower and the Seed: the parable of the Good Shepherd with his lost sheep: the parable of the Prodigal Son. In reading the Scriptures I find miracles. I need to read those miracles and not to push them aside. I need to believe them! They show me God is Almighty! They indicate the things of God are beyond this world: Almighty God is supernatural. God has power, and when I read those miracles I can feel it. As I read, I need to keep my mind open. The Scriptures will feed me and bless me, and so I will grow in faith. I should read with an open mind and pray with a humble spirit, that I might reach conclusions for the present. Tomorrow I will learn more. And as surely as I read the Word of God blessing will be upon me. "Blessed are they which hear and those which read the words of this prophecy." "Whatsoever things were written aforetime were written for our learning, that we through patience and comfort of the Scriptures might have hope."

39.

Chastening and Spiritual Growth

Can you understand how suffering pain and having trouble can actually result in a stronger spiritual life?

Our interest in these studies is spiritual living. We want to understand what it means to live in faith in the Lord and be blessed. Some people have trouble. But if you are trusting and believing in God, having confessed your sin, and having admitted that you do not always do everything right, and that you are totally dependent upon His mercy, why should you have trouble? In answer we note first a word from Jesus of Nazareth Himself: "Every branch that beareth fruit, he purgeth it, that it may bring forth more fruit" (John 15:2). When the word "purge" is used as in this context in referring to fruit trees it means "prune" the trees. The purpose of this process is to cut away the unnecessary branches. Persons who tend to fruitbearing trees know about pruning. Keeping a garden one would know about hoeing weeds.

A similar truth is operative in spiritual affairs. In the parable of the Sower and the Seed there were four different kinds of soil, including the thorny ground. When seed fell there it sprang up because that was good soil, but there were thistles and thorns. The thorns sprang up and choked the plants, so the seed did not produce fruit.

The problem of the Christian arises in the reality of the two worlds. Paul pointed out the two bodies a Christian has:

> It is sown a natural body; it is raised a spiritual body. There is a natural body, and there is a spiritual body (I Corinthians 15:44).

The Christian lives as a human being in the natural world, and being born again as a child of God he also lives in the spiritual world. This sets up a conflict. Paul speaks of the words "flesh and spirit." And Paul uses such terms as "carnal" for the one and "spiritual" for the other. Blessing with joy is for the spiritual, but the Christian begins living in the natural. It is when he accepts Christ, that he is born again in the spiritual. This new life, the spiritual, must be fostered and nurtured through the Word of God. "As newborn babes, desire the sincere milk of the word, that ye may grow thereby" (I Peter 2:2).

The spiritual life of a Christian is grounded in his faith. But faith is not constant. I can have more faith and I can have less faith. My faith can be stronger and my faith can be weaker, and this makes a difference in the way I live. In order that plants may become fruitful, and then to be more fruitful, certain things can be done. In the garden we dig up the ground, fertilize it, and irrigate it so that the plants will grow. My own experience with my garden caused me often to say, "I think I am growing the best weeds in the county." I would put plant food in the soil and the weeds would grow until they became bigger and bigger. The weeds needed to be cut out. The procedure for producing food in the garden is to feed that which is good and to cut out that which is evil. This is exactly the procedure followed in spiritual living. Spiritually we feed the spirit and crucify the flesh.

Jesus of Nazareth told His disciples to expect trouble because this was the way of the Father in promoting spiritual living. Trouble would come, but they should endure trouble with hope. He said, "If the world hate you, ye know it hated me before it hated you." Then again He told them on another occasion, "In the world ye shall have tribulation: but be of good cheer; I have overcome the world" (John 16:33).

Trouble will come because Christians are in the world, but because they are believers they will be able to overcome it. God will overrule all trouble so as to bring His will to pass. The lesson in all this is both simple and profound. A Christian person has the flesh, or human nature, and he has the Spirit, that is the new life, within him. The flesh needs to be controlled and denied; the Spirit needs to be fed and cultured. The flesh is to be crucified so as to put it to death; and the Spirit is to be fed, that it might grow.

The believer is asked to control his body by yielding it into the will of God; but the actual putting to death of the self is the work of God. In the putting of the self to death, the believer must be willing that this should be done. It is true he must yield himself, but he need not do this to himself. This will be done by the will of God and is the work of God. Often God's way of getting this done is to allow trouble. Trouble will mortify the self, and the trouble that crucifies the flesh is usually at the hands of other persons, even friends.

> Verily, verily, I say unto thee, When thou wast young, thou girdest thyself, and walkedst whither thou wouldest: but when thou shalt be old, thou shalt stretch forth thy hands, and another shall gird thee, and carry thee whither thou wouldest not. This spake he, signifying by what death he should glorify God. And when he had spoken this, he saith unto him, Follow me (John 21:18-19).

The Lord was crucified by soldiers, unbelievers, and this demonstrated the truth of Romans 8:28. God is able to make all things work together for good to them that love God. Because this is true Paul could say that he gloried in tribulation.

Why is it then that some people have more suffering than others? Suffering experiences are like the heat of the oven that bakes the apple. Sometimes when apples are baked they are sweeter. But it is well to remember "It just takes some apples longer to bake through than it does others."

40.

Basic Assumptions in Praying

Do you realize that a person must believe certain things about God to be able to pray sincerely?

> But without faith it is impossible to please him: for he that cometh to God must believe that he is, and that he is a rewarder of them that diligently seek him (Hebrews 11:6).

This is the way in which it is plainly stated in the book of Hebrews, and we are reminded of this when we come to pray. I can understand why some men do not pray. They are honest, but I think they're wrong. If a man does not believe there is a God, he would be a liar and a hypocrite to take part in praying. And if a man had no idea of the promises of God, he would have no basis on which to ask for anything. Much praying is doubtless generated by the need that we feel, the distress that we're in, the desires that we have. Such praying is a good deal like saying "Ouch!" That's genuine enough but it is pointless. "God is, and is a rewarder of them that diligently seek him." This is true but so largely ignored.

When we pray there must be some basic conviction in our soul that will guide our thoughts and sustain our requests when we come before God. God is a living Person. We can come to Him with confidence. He is everything I am as a Person, and so much more. Whatever I have, He has more; and as much as I'm aware of what is going on, He knows more of what is going on. If I know of someone who needs help, He knows more. In Jesus, He became incarnate and the Lord Jesus could say, "He that hath seen me hath seen the Father."

The Gospel records of Matthew, Mark, Luke and John, show

160

clearly that anybody could come to Jesus of Nazareth at any time and open his heart to ask for anything, and He would hear him.

He is alive now and can hear my cry. He is a Person and can act. One of the first things I need to have in mind when I am praying is that God is right by me. I don't have to go to find Him; He is right here! I don't have to touch Him to turn His attention to me. This living God, who is right here with us, knows everything. He knows what I have need of before I ask. He knows that I am helpless to do anything about it. He knows that I cannot work my way out of the situation I am in. And He knows just how heavy the load may be upon me.

I was recently reading one of the letters we received at our office, and noted the request for prayer from a certain woman. As my wife and I read that request we were deeply touched. She said very simply: "The doctor says I have cancer. Please pray for my husband and children." We were touched by that, but it was a blessing to remember about Almighty God. God knew about that cancer and God knew about that husband and about those children. He wants us to call upon Him; He wants us to talk to Him; but He knows. When I go before God to pray, I may not even know the full extent of what I need, but God knows! God is good! I mean to say He is kind, He is merciful; He is a God of compassion. I need to remind my heart He wants to help me. He will receive me when I come to Him. I do not have to intrude on Him. I do not have to go through any receptionist at a desk to get a chance to go in and talk to Him. He is right at hand, and He is gracious. "Whosoever will" may come to God. God is no respecter of persons. While it is true I can come to Him, I have no ground to stand on. There is no point in me spreading out before you all my shortcomings and weaknesses. I can assure you I could not stand before God in myself; but I can come. I have disobeyed Him. He knows that very well, better than I do. I have disregarded Him. It isn't only that there have been times that I've thought about Him and turned away, but sometimes I can forget Him. Then it is not just a matter of disregarding Him, but of not even thinking about Him. But God is gracious. He will receive me.

And though I don't deserve it, He will look to see if He can help me. He will turn to me. This is the floor of faith on which we can walk.

God is good! God really wants to help you. He really is compassionate. And God is gracious. "Whosoever will may come." God is Almighty! He is able! The Bible in one place asks the question, "Is there anything too hard for the Lord?" The angel Gabriel told Mary, "Nothing is impossible with God." Jesus in speaking to His disciples said, "With God all things are possible." You may count on this in your heart and cherish it in your very soul: God can! He is able. No matter what my problem, no matter what my need, He is able to do more than I can ask or think. Whatever your situation may be, you may keep in mind: God can! God is sovereign. He is Lord over all; He is on the Throne, stated simply: God is Boss! He controls the world. When I turn to God, I'm turning to the One who can, who will, and who wants to help me.

41.

Examples of Praying in Scripture

Have you any idea as to why anyone would pray to the invisible God for help in a practical situation here on earth?

If a person were living truly as a Christian, how could he ask for help when God cannot be seen? We could understand why one would go to a doctor, or a member of the family, or perhaps a neighbor for help, but why go to God? He's invisible. How is He involved with what is going on here? The Bible indicates that He is. Not only is it true that God is Almighty and that He can do as He will, but the record in the Bible shows that in the course of time many believing people have called on God and they have been heard. The Bible tells about one after another who turned to God in his or her need, and was helped. It's not surprising that a person who is in need would cry out for help, but why should that person turn to God?

Basic to the idea that would cause a person to turn to God is a covenant, a promise that God made to Abraham and his seed. He said to Israel, "Call upon me, and I will answer thee, and show thee great and mighty things" (Jeremiah 33:3). In response to this sort of an invitation believing persons have turned to God. The history of God's people has recorded in the Bible many instances of such praying. Let us consider first of all Abraham, particularly the situation that arose when God revealed to Abraham that He was going to destroy the city of Sodom. Abraham's nephew, Lot, was in the city of Sodom, which could have prompted Abraham to pray that Sodom might be spared. Genesis 18 is the rather long and detailed report of how Abraham talked with God in prayer on behalf of the city of Sodom, making intercession for it. The city wasn't spared, but Lot was delivered. When the godly man Abraham saw that

Sodom was to be destroyed, he went to God in prayer. This example shows intercession is proper. I should pray for you. You should pray for me. We should pray for others. We should pray for our pastor, our families, our community, for our government. We should pray for blessing in our practical situations.

Now let us look at the case of Jacob. The Bible tells us that Jacob deceived his father and secured the blessing that was intended for Esau. We read that Esau was so angry about it that he sought to kill Jacob. Jacob ran away from home to live with his uncle where he stayed for twenty years. There he married, had children, and became wealthy. When he was returning home he was told that his brother Esau, whom he had offended twenty years before, was coming with four hundred soldiers. This filled Jacob with an understandable dread. Now he is a man facing a perilous situation, in grave danger of losing everything, including his life. But he is a believing man and he goes to God in prayer. Jacob's praying took the form of wrestling with a messenger from God, with whom he wrestled all through the night until dawn was breaking. We learn in that dramatic account that the important aspect in praying is persistence: staying with it, continuing to wait upon God. Jacob's famous words, "I will not let thee go except thou bless me" are a classic form of the cry that should come up from our hearts.

Again, we may think about Moses. There are many instances in the story of Moses where he talked with God. Praying was something Moses did often. Yet, of all the events in Moses' career, one outstanding event was his experience on Mount Sinai, when he received the law of God written on the tables of stone. While there he received the pattern of the tabernacle. Also during the forty days there, he received guidance as to the function and duties of the priests as well as the whole pattern of the ritual for the religious services that were to be conducted in the tabernacle. Moses was leading the people out of Egypt but he had no idea that he knew enough to do this in his own strength or wisdom. He looked to God for guidance, spending forty days in prayer waiting on God.

There is another remarkable instance in the record of Moses

sending Joshua to lead the forces of Israel against Amalek. In the actual battle Amalek was stronger than Israel and would have defeated Israel, but Moses went to the mountain to pray, lifting up his hands to God. As long as Moses' hands stayed up in prayer Joshua would win. But Moses grew tired and his hands became heavy, so they would come down. When they did, Joshua began to lose. At this point Aaron and Hur came and held up the hands of Moses until the going down of the sun. Joshua won a notable victory; Moses was involved in it because of his praying, but the margin of victory was in Aaron and Hur. These two men held up the hands of Moses, helping him by praying. This is a notable example of the power and the function of united intercessory praying. "The Bible for You" ministry is supported by a group of volunteers who pray for this work. These supporters are called the A & H Club. That name is given to all who indicate they will pray for their pastor and for the radio ministry. They are called the Aaron and Hur Club, the A & H Club, because they hold up the hands of those who broadcast the message of the gospel, and also the hands of their pastor.

Over and over the record shows that Moses turned to God for help. Regardless of our problems, we should turn to God in prayer. Just because we have trouble doesn't mean we are on the wrong road. We may be right, exactly where God wants us to be, and yet need to cry out to Him for help and strength. In such cases we can have help from each other.

Another instance of praying would be Hannah's request. She was the mother of Samuel. She prayed earnestly to God for a child. Her deep concern was a very personal matter. She was at a disadvantage in comparison to another woman because she had no child. In her trouble she went to God. She believed God could help, so she went to Him and asked Him to do something about it. The wonderful fact was that God did. Samuel was born as a result. From this we can learn that when we are in personal need, we could come to God and seek His face with confidence.

There are many other instances of praying recorded in the Old Testament. The Scriptures tell about Elijah when he was on Mount

Carmel, praying for rain. Truly "the effectual fervent prayer of a righteous man availeth much." When Solomon was called to be king he humbly went before God and asked Him for wisdom, which he received. Daniel, in a foreign country, receiving visions from God, prayed to God for understanding. It was given to him.

There is one example which should give us warning. When Hezekiah, the king, was told by the prophet that his days were up, that he should get himself ready to die, he turned his face to the wall and wept. He wanted to live longer. God gave him more time, fifteen years, during which time Hezekiah did the only foolish thing told about him, and actually brought a blemish to his record. This is sobering: to see that a believing man can be led by his own wishes to pray to God for that which is foolish. God granted his request, even though it was not His first choice for him.

42.

Praying in the Church

Do you realize that the Bible teaches that Christians should gather together and pray together for blessing?

"For where two or three are gathered together in my name, there am I in the midst of them." These familiar words are found in Matthew 18:20. They plainly say that the Lord Himself in our hearts will guide us into His will when we are praying together as believers. One of the first principles learned by the Christian in living by faith is that he is not alone. The design in creation is that it is not good for a man to be alone. Sin breaks this fellowship and arouses animosity. Sin brings suspicion of each other. It is wonderful to realize that grace is greater than sin, and brings reconciliation, trust and brotherly interest. The gospel leads into fellowship. As I yield myself to the Lord, look to Him and come to Him, I find that I come with others who also look to the Lord, trusting in Him; thus we have communion with each other. We are fellow believers and our communion extends even into the exercise of praying.

There are several instances recorded in the New Testament which show us what can be learned about praying together. When Peter and John had been arrested for preaching, and were brought before the authorities, the court accused them of violating the orders that had been given to them and warned them not to preach any more in the name of Jesus Christ. The record is that Peter stood up and boldly challenged them to judge whether a person should obey God or man, and then declared that so far as he and John were concerned, being servants of God, they could only do what they had been commanded to do by Him. The court warned them again and released them.

So when they had further threatened them, they let them go,

167

finding nothing how they might punish them, because of the
people: for all men glorified God for that which was done. For
the man was above forty years old, on whom this miracle of
healing was showed. And being let go, they went to their own
company, and reported all that the chief priests and elders had
said unto them (Acts 4:21-23).

Thus Peter and John went back to the church and shared with the
other Christians what the situation was.

And when they heard that, they lifted up their voice to God
with one accord, and said, Lord, thou art God, which hast
made heaven, and earth, and the sea, and all that in them is:
who by the mouth of thy servant David hast said, Why did the
heathen rage, and the people imagine vain things? The kings of
the earth stood up, and the rulers were gathered together
against the Lord, and against his Christ (Acts 4:24-26).

In this way they brought to mind Scripture that outlined the very
kind of situation they were facing, the very kind of opposition that
they had, and so were strengthened to continue:

For of a truth against thy holy child Jesus, whom thou hast
anointed, both Herod, and Pontius Pilate, with the Gentiles,
and the people of Israel, were gathered together, for to do
whatsoever thy hand and thy counsel determined before to be
done (Acts 4:27-28).

This incident records how the disciples in praying recalled what
the Scriptures said so that they might know that the situation they
were in was not unusual. This was the way it would be with believers.
What was happening to them was evidence that the prophecy which
God had revealed about conditions in this world was actually being
fulfilled. This strengthened them in their prayer, "And now, Lord,
behold their threatenings: and grant unto thy servants, that with all
boldness they may speak thy word" (Acts 4:29).

There is another profound lesson to learn. When these Spirit-led
disciples were encouraged by Scripture to ask God for help they did

not request that God strike their persecutors dead. Nor did they request that their opponents should be changed. Someone might suggest "Why not pray for those enemies of yours that they be different?" These disciples did not ask, "O God, work a miracle in their hearts and make them all nice people." These authorities were threatening them. They threatened to beat them. The disciples were facing brutal suffering, but they prayed "Grant unto thy servants, that with all boldness they may speak thy word." When believers face trouble they call on God to take them through, not to remove the trouble. When the waters come up high as a flood, the believer does not pray Almighty God to remove the flood, but that God will be with him and lead him through the flood! This is so vital it should be shouted into our ears.

Let us review this important truth. The early church had been told to preach. God commanded them to witness. They were to tell everybody. The authorities of the day said, "You must not preach." These Christians turned to God to pray for help. They did not ask Almighty God, "Change the hearts of those people." Nor did they ask, "Wipe all those people out." Neither did they pray Almighty God, "Send us a group of soldiers to defend us." They expected trouble. They intended to endure that trouble and they called on Almighty God for just one blessing: "Make us strong to go through for him." There was no attempt to avoid the threatened trouble; they just wanted grace to face the consequences. It is thrilling to read, "And when they had prayed, the place was shaken where they were assembled together; and they were all filled with the Holy Ghost, and they spake the word of God with boldness" (Acts 4:31).

Later in their affairs when the disciples had continued to shock the community with preaching the truth that Jesus of Nazareth was alive, Peter was put into prison, and the order went out that he was to be put to death.

> Now about that time Herod the king stretched forth his hands to vex certain of the church. And he killed James the brother of John with the sword. And because he saw it pleased the Jews, he proceeded further to take Peter also. . . . And when

he had apprehended him, he put him in prison, and delivered him to four quaternions of soldiers to keep him; intending after Easter to bring him forth to the people. Peter therefore was kept in prison: but prayer was made without ceasing of the church unto God for him (Acts 12:1-5).

For what would you think the church prayed? Consider how Jesus prayed for Peter: "And the Lord said, Simon, Simon, behold, Satan hath desired to have you, that he may sift you as wheat: but I have prayed for thee, that thy faith fail not" (Luke 22:31-32). There was no request for a change of circumstances! There was no request that Satan be changed or destroyed. There was only request for strength to persevere. It would be no lack of faith if the church expected him to be killed. James had been killed. Peter was no better than James. As a matter of fact the Lord had predicted that Peter would die for Him (John 21:19). These fellow believers shared Peter's predicament and no doubt prayed for him to have strength to endure. There was a miraculous deliverance, but it seems to have been unexpected and probably unasked for. This simply demonstrates that when believers pray the results can often be more than they could ask or think.

It is inspiring to note in these incidents that at first there was no hostility toward opponents. These Spirit-led believers intended no harm to their opponents. Their conduct seems to reflect what happened on Calvary when the Lord said, "Father, forgive them, for they know not what they do." We may recall how Stephen said, "Lord, lay not this sin to their charge." Then there was no withdrawal because of danger. No stopping! No turning back! No quitting! Just humble yielding into the will of God. This is the way God leads His people. As Christians we should ask, "Give us the strength, give us the grace, that we may go forward." Then we may proceed with triumphant confidence in God. If God will be for us, no one can be against us.

43.

Praying as a Form of Service

Can you see how praying would be a form of real service?

"Moreover as for me, God forbid that I should sin against the Lord in ceasing to pray for you" (I Samuel 12:23). These are the words spoken by Samuel to the children of Israel. Samuel had been a great good judge. When he became old, the people came to him and asked him for a king. Samuel warned them that having a king could bring trouble. Through the king there would be oppression. Nevertheless they wanted a king. God told Samuel to give them a king. Samuel told the people that because God said he should do so, he would select a king for them. But he also outlined what God said would happen to the people, and concluded his remarks with these amazing words, "Moreover as for me, God forbid that I should sin against the Lord in ceasing to pray for you." In other words Samuel said: "You are about to do wrong. You have made a bad choice. It will not turn out well for you, but God forbid that I should sin in ceasing to pray for you even if you are going on the wrong road. And I will teach you the good and the right way." This incident illustrates an important truth.

In this world men need help. The Scriptures report some instances that help in understanding what can be done.

There was a time when Abraham was concerned about the city of Sodom. Abraham and his nephew Lot had traveled along together for awhile and then because of trouble among their servants they had separated. Abraham gave Lot his choice to go in one direction while he, Abraham, would go in the other. Lot looked the situation over and saw a very good area with plenty of good pastureland, well-watered, down by the River Jordan, which was close to the city of Sodom. Later he was in Sodom when it was captured by the enemy. When Abraham heard about this, he went to rescue Lot and had succeeded in restoring him. God told Abraham He intended to destroy Sodom. Abraham approached God concerning His will and providence and prayed. When a believer seeks the help of God he prays.

Another instance occurred when Moses was on Mount Sinai. While Moses was on the Mount it was revealed to him that the people had made a golden calf in order to worship it. This was sinful and Moses knew that God would judge them. Moses himself judged them, but when he was finished with chastising them, and correcting their attitude in a violent way, he went to pray to God that He should forgive the people. They had done wrong. They were on the wrong road and Moses had judged them for it, but then he goes to God and prays for them. They needed the forgiveness of God and for this Moses prayed:

> Oh, this people have sinned a great sin, and have made them gods of gold. Yet now, if thou wilt forgive their sin—; and if not, blot me, I pray thee, out of thy book which thou hast written (Exodus 32:31-32).

These are wonderful examples to any believer when dealing with other people.

It will always be true when we want the blessing of God on other people, that we should pray. In this way we are serving other people. Abraham served Lot by praying about Sodom. Moses served his people by praying that God would forgive them. Samuel served Israel by praying that God would give them wisdom to know how to act when they had a king.

This was the case with Ezra. Ezra was one of the leaders of the people when they came back from Babylon to Jerusalem. Ezra was serving in setting up the worship of God and teaching the people about the law of God. Unknown to him the people had fallen into sin. Ezra knew that God had chastened these people in the course of their history. But the people were incorrigible and now they had sinned again. Ezra was deeply smitten about this. He had no heart to pray to God (Ezra 9:14-15). A layman came to Ezra and said, "There is still hope about this. You go ahead and ask God. We'll straighten ourselves up. We will change our ways, but you pray for us." Thus Ezra was encouraged by one of the laymen to exercise his faith in intercession for the people. God could forgive them, and God could overrule, but this would come in answer to prayer. Ezra prayed and God forgave them.

In the New Testament it is written how Jesus was teaching on one occasion:

> But when he saw the multitudes, he was moved with compassion on them, because they fainted, and were scattered abroad, as sheep having no shepherd. Then saith he unto his disciples, The harvest truly is plenteous, but the laborers are few; pray ye therefore the Lord of the harvest, that he will send forth laborers into his harvest (Matthew 9:36-38).

This is very significant! He did not urge these people to be organized. They were without a shepherd, and they fainted because of the weariness of their actual living experiences. What they needed was the grace and blessing of God. They needed ministers and missionaries among them to tell them about God. This illustrates the great truth that the real call to do anything for the Lord must come from within, from the heart. God will put it there in answer to prayer. When we see anyone seeking to win another to the Lord, we can be sure that somewhere someone is praying that God will thrust forth laborers into His harvest. Paul says, "Woe is me if I preach not the gospel." God puts such burden in the heart, and God will do this in answer to prayer. This truth helps in understanding Acts 6:4. Here Peter is telling the people they should have somebody supervising the handing out of the gifts to the poor. They should not count on the apostles to do this. "But we will give ourselves continually to prayer and to the ministry of the Word." The apostle is saying that in the actual work of the ministry praying is most important.

44.

Significance of Praying in the Will of God

Have you ever realized why praying with understanding is so important?

> Ye lust, and have not: ye kill, and desire to have, and cannot obtain: ye fight and war, yet ye have not, because ye ask not. Ye ask, and receive not, because ye ask amiss, that ye may consume it upon your lusts (James 4:2-3).

It is a common idea about praying to think we should ask for whatever we want, especially if it's beyond our reach. If it is within our reach we should go and get it. But this is not true. The believer should come to God about everything! He should ask God for His will to be done as he prays. God holds all in His hands. It is to be feared, that believers often feel that the promises of God are unlimited and unconditional. Did not God say He would do anything if the believer would ask Him? This mistaken idea leads to disappointment which in turn weakens faith. The promises of God are all lined up according to His will. There are some people who ask and do not receive. There are others who do without because they do not ask.

There is a widespread confidence in praying, since commonly speaking men do believe in prayer. There is no other exercise of the soul that is so universally commended by all. A look at the Scriptural record of the lives of godly men and women reveals they were all praying people. Commandments have been given by God, as a divine injunction to pray. The Apostle Paul writes to Timothy: "I will therefore that men pray everywhere" (I Timothy 2:8). Jesus taught that men ought always to pray and not to faint. The teaching of the New Testament, as of the Bible as a whole, encourages prayer. The prophetic word was "Call upon me and I will answer thee and

174

show thee great and mighty things thou knowest not of." Such promises direct the praying of the people. Jesus, the Son of God, set the example. One thing that marked His life was that He spent time in prayer; on occasion He would spend all night in prayer. Christian experience in the history of the church has verified a million times over that God hears and answers prayer.

There are common ways of praying when you have fellowship with the Lord. Some people when they get up in the morning pause to ask God to bless them that day. Some make it a practice when they sit down to the table at any one of their meals to give thanks to God for their food. Some at night when they go to bed will kneel and pray to God. Sometimes families get together to read the Bible and have prayer. That means daily fellowship with the Lord.

Another common form of praying is to pray for our loved ones, especially for those that are absent. When young people go off to college, parents pray for them. When young people go on vacation, families pray for them. When a man leaves home to go on a business trip, others will pray for him. Whenever there is uncertainty it is common to pray. In any kind of danger we pray. If we fear for the safety of loved ones we pray. If we have a strong desire that loved ones should be well taken care of, we will pray for them. It is common to pray when you are in trouble. If you are inclined to be hopeless about things, when it looks as if there's no way out, you can always look up: God is able. There is nothing impossible with God. You could be downhearted and in trouble. You could always look up! You could call upon God! In situations with crises, danger, uncertainty, it is common for a Christian to turn to God and pray, "Oh Lord, help me now!"

We thank God for all such privileges, but our praying can be more than that! Sometimes people look upon praying as a kind of tax payment. It seems as if they were paying insurance premiums on their eternal life. They want to be sure they are going to get to heaven, so they'll pray some. In such cases the believer will pray less and less, because he finds out he can get by with less. For some praying is sort of an ejaculation; something hurts and they say,

"Ouch!" When it stops hurting they stop praying. Some in desperation say, "Well, I'll try anything. I'll even pray." Now all of this is very well, and I wouldn't say that this is unworthy altogether; but it is not enough.

Why don't I pray more? Often it's ignorance, or indifference, or I am just plain lazy. Sometimes the reason I don't pray is it's so much bother and it makes me tired. I go to sleep when I pray. Then again it may be irresponsibility. A person can feel about a problem: it doesn't bother me. In that case he will not pray. Sometimes sin hurts too much to pray. When I bow down before God, I even get on my knees before God, I just don't feel good. Another reason why we don't pray more is impatience. It takes too long. You ask and you ask and you ask and God has not acted promptly when you asked. Sometimes it takes time for God to work out His plan and then there are those of us who just get impatient. We are not going to wait.

There is something else I want to point out and it will not be easy to describe. I may not pray because of my irreligious intimacies. There is no use to cover up this condition in a nice sugar coating. When the company we keep, the folks we run around with are not praying people we don't pray. They're unbelieving people so we don't believe. Our companions, the books we read, the thoughts we have, all these are forms of unbelief. And unbelief disqualifies a person who wants to pray. Truly, "Ye ask, and receive not, because ye ask amiss."

45.

Unanswered Prayer

Do you realize that sometimes prayers will be unanswered?

Much praying that goes on is superficial and not practical. That is very unfortunate. Perhaps we do not always realize that the spiritual tone of the praying person makes a difference. The strength of faith that the praying person has actually matters in having his prayers effectual. This is to be seen when looking at the problem of unanswered prayer. I remember when I was a pastor, announcing one Sunday that the following Sunday I would preach on "Unanswered Prayer." That afternoon a mother called me up to tell me that her high school daughter had been in church that morning and was greatly disturbed when she heard that the pastor was planning to talk on "Unanswered Prayer": in her understanding there was no "unanswered prayer." Then I had the task of telling this mother that her very earnest and very interested young daughter just did not know what the Bible taught, because the Bible does actually deal with unanswered prayer.

As a result of what that mother said, I made a special study throughout the Bible during that week, on the one subject of prayer. I discovered that the greater part of unanswered prayer is really unheard prayer. It is not only true that God doesn't always answer, but it actually is true that God does not always hear. The very idea of that would be a shock to many people. They assume God would be sure to listen. But as a matter of fact, He outlines very definite conditions under which He will not hear when men call on Him. The general cause is sin. Scripture says plainly, "Thy word have I hid in my heart that I might not sin against thee."

Sin disqualifies the soul from receiving answers, such as the refusal to hear God's Word. It is written: "If they will not heed my word, neither will I heed their cry when they call unto me." If a man will not read the Bible, and so will not pay attention to the Word of God, God has revealed He will not pay attention to him when he cries out in prayer.

Another reason for unanswered prayer is put in these words: "If you are deaf to the cry of the poor." This means just what it says: if a man will not hear the poor when they cry, God will not hear him. It is such an easy thing for me to turn my back to the poor. I need not be surprised if God turns His back on me! I know it is not my fault that there are poor people. I did not make them poor, but they are poor. As a matter of fact I will not meet all the poor people in the world. But I will meet some. And some of these poor people that I meet are my personal responsibility. In the parable of the Good Samaritan I can be sure that God saw how the priest walked by on the other side, and the Levite walked by on the other side. Also God Almighty saw when the Good Samaritan went down to that poor man in the ditch and helped him.

Another hindrance to receiving blessing is an unforgiving spirit. I will be disqualified to receive blessing if I do not forgive. Jesus of Nazareth taught: "Forgive us our debts as we forgive our debtors." If any man will not forgive his brother his trespasses, neither will the Father forgive him his trespasses. If I bring my gift to the altar and there remember that my brother hath ought against me, I should leave there my gift; go and be reconciled to my brother first. If I do not forgive my brother God will not hear me.

We have noted now three conditions which will disqualify me from being heard when I pray: refusal to hear God's Word so that I do not pay attention to the Bible; deaf to the cry of the poor so that I do not pay any attention to the poor; and if I do not forgive my brother when he injures me.

But there's more! Jesus told about the two men who went up to the temple to pray. One man said, "I thank thee God, that I'm not as other men are, as this poor man standing here. I tithe all I possess and I give, I attend the services, I go to the temple and worship. I bring in my sacrifices." The other man durst not lift up his eyes unto heaven, but smote upon his breast and said, "God be merciful to me a sinner." Jesus said that the second man went down to his house justified rather than the first one. God knows the hearts of all who come to pray. A humble and contrite heart the Lord will not despise. As long as I am proud I need not talk or mouth any prayers. They will not go any higher than the ceiling.

The Bible reveals about the Moabites that because they served other gods, God would not listen to them when they prayed (Isaiah 16:12). When my interest is in other things than in God, He will not hear me!

Some prayers are unanswered. In the story of the rich man and Lazarus, both died: Lazarus went to be in Abraham's bosom and the rich man went to hell. The rich man in hell prayed to Abraham and asked Abraham to send someone to talk to his brothers. But his request was not granted. A person can wait until it is too late. When once a soul passes out of this world, he will find a great gulf fixed between those accepted and those rejected. Those rejected have no way to come to God to be blessed.

Another condition that will result in prayer not being answered is the matter of being selfish. James wrote, "Ye ask, and receive not, because ye ask amiss" (James 4:3). Some will say about praying that God is so good He will answer anybody. This is not true. God is gracious, but He will not give everybody that asks anything he may want. When the mother of Zebedee's children came to Jesus of Nazareth and asked Him for the privilege that one of her sons should sit on His right hand while the other sat on His left as they came into the Kingdom, she did not get her request. She prayed, but she was selfish: she did not get her request.

There is also the matter of unbelief. The disciples were distressed that when they had prayed that the boy should be delivered from demons, it did not happen (Matthew 17:19-20). The record states that the father brought the boy to the apostles, and asked them to pray for him. They did, but the spirit did not leave the boy. Later Jesus of Nazareth cast him out. The disciples earnestly came to Him and asked, "Why couldn't we do it?" And He said, "Because of your unbelief." It is obvious that unbelief disqualifies a person when he prays. A famous instance of an unanswered prayer occurred when David had committed his sin with Bathsheba, and she gave birth to his child. When the child fell sick, David went to pray. All the time the child was sick David did not take off his clothes: he stayed up day and night, and prayed. He would not eat; he would not shave; he prayed day and night, but the child died. God had said the child would die. David's prayer was directly contrary to the will of God. And if the request is contrary to the will of God it will not be granted.

There are two other famous instances. On one occasion in the Old Testament Moses had offended God. He had committed sin and God told him because of this he would never enter into the land. Moses said afterwards that he asked God three times to let him enter Canaan, but God said, "Speak to me no more on this matter." Moses knew why he did not get permission to enter, but his prayer request remained unanswered. The Bible tells about Paul being troubled with his thorn in the flesh. Paul wrote about this to say he had asked again and again that the Father would deliver him, but the word came to him from God that the thorn was there for a purpose. It was not in the will of God to remove that thorn in the flesh from His servant, Paul. Both Moses and Paul knew why their prayer was denied; neither one of them ever blamed God.

All of these instances of unanswered prayer: when it is too late; when you are selfish; when you are full of unbelief; when you are praying for something contrary to God's expressed will, or something not in the will of God; all this was known in New Testament times, and yet believers had confidence in God, and they received answers to prayer. Jesus Himself said that if anybody asked for something to be done in His Name, He would do it. The whole issue seems to be whether or not the praying is in His Name. If it is in His Name, He will do it. This means to say if the request is in keeping with what Christ Jesus came into the world to do; if the request is along that line you can be very sure that it will be answered. If it is not along that line, you have no promise from God about it. We must be humbly willing to do God's will. Then God will hear and answer.

46.

The Function of the Holy Spirit

Did you know that God has made complete arrangements to make sure that all who believe in Him will be kept in His will?

"And I will pray the Father, and he shall give you another Comforter." These are the words of Jesus as He was speaking to His disciples on the last occasion He was alone with them. This time of private fellowship is reported in John 13—17. In John 14:16-18 we read:

> And I will pray the Father, and he shall give you another Comforter, that he may abide with you for ever; even the Spirit of truth; whom the world cannot receive, because it seeth him not, neither knoweth him: but ye know him; for he dwelleth with you, and shall be in you. I will not leave you comfortless: I will come to you.

A little later in 16:12-14 we read:

> I have yet many things to say unto you, but ye cannot bear them now. Howbeit when he, the Spirit of truth, is come, he will guide you into all truth: for he shall not speak of himself; but whatsoever he shall hear, that shall he speak: and he will show you things to come. He shall glorify me: for he shall receive of mine, and shall show it unto you.

This is how the Lord Jesus prepared His disciples to expect that God was going to send the Holy Spirit to be with them and to live with them. The Christian is a person who has accepted Jesus Christ as his Savior and Lord, and by the grace of God has been born again; he is now a new creation, ambitious to be well pleasing in the sight of God.

The Holy Spirit is vital for the Christian. It is written: "Whosoever doeth the will of God abideth forever." The will of God is eternal. The will of God makes certain demands upon man, which are hard to accept.

Usually when we are almost in despair, and because we cannot do anything else, we may yield ourselves into God's hands. It is always hard to choose to do the will of God because this leads us to deny ourselves.

Part of the problem is the sinfulness of man, which every child of Adam shares by birth. This nature of man as a child of Adam is a barrier to his fellowship with God. When any man turns to God he senses his guilt and realizes his wrongdoing. The human heart is naturally sinful. The prophets wrote about this, saying that the heart is sinful beyond belief, and desperately wicked. Man is naturally selfish, proud and lazy. Man is also weak. Because all this is true man needs the help of the Holy Spirit to do the will of God that he might be blessed.

How can one understand that God is all merciful when He allows trouble? How can one believe that God is all powerful when wicked men are able to do wickedly and prosper? Such things make it hard to accept that God is on the throne; and even if one has had experiences of blessing from God it is hard to remember them. It is so easy to forget what God did yesterday. Man always finds it difficult to respond to the will of God when this involves his self-denial. But this is unavoidable: "If any man will come after me, let him deny himself, take up his cross and follow me." The believer must be willing to commit himself into the will of God even though it means death to self. Being yielded to God means that God will work in the believer to will and to do of His good pleasure. To choose to yield is a difficult thing for a man to do. A person might be inclined that way on a particular Sunday, but by Tuesday he will have forgotten it, because man is weak. The Holy Spirit would enable us to do it.

If I walk the ways of God to do His will I will have to do without certain things. The Bible would teach me to trust God and yield to

Him, and to take joyfully the spoiling of my goods. This is set forth in the truth of the gospel and made possible by the coming of the Holy Spirit. In Christ we have His grace.

> For ye know the grace of our Lord Jesus Christ, that, though he was rich, yet for your sakes he became poor, that ye through his poverty might be rich (II Corinthians 8:9).

I am reminded of a lifeguard standing on the shore. If someone swimming gets into trouble and seems to be in danger of drowning, the lifeguard's duty is to go into the water after him. That is what Christ Jesus did. He was in heaven with His Father; but He left heaven and came to earth that He might be "touched with all the feelings of our infirmities." The Son of God died on Calvary's cross that He might save us. He believed that His Fahter would raise Him from the dead and would give Him all those who put their trust in Him. This is the grace of Christ, who came to save dying souls. God is gracious, and He is powerful. He raised the body of Jesus Christ from the dead. He is able to save to the uttermost those that come unto Him through Jesus Christ, because He is able to raise from the dead those who believe in Him and give to them His Holy Spirit.

When God worked with Moses, He did not cause Pharaoh to drop dead. He gave Moses strength to do His will. This is how the power of God works, and this is what the Holy Spirit brings to us. The plan of God is to provide believers with a Guide who will guide them. He does not give a rule book: He sends a Guide. God does not give a set of instructions as to how to get well: He sends a Doctor. He sends a Friend to be with us. The Holy Spirit will take the things of the Lord Jesus Christ and show them to the believer. The plan of God is that the believer is to be helped into His will by "Christ in you, the hope of glory."

47.

Significance in Pentecost

Would you understand why Pentecost is so meaningful to Christians?

> I indeed baptize you with water unto repentance: but he that cometh after me is mightier than I, whose shoes I am not worthy to bear: he shall baptize you with the Holy Ghost, and with fire (Matthew 3:11).

These words were spoken by John the Baptist as he went about preaching. Many people had been so impressed with him when they came to hear him, that some of them thought that he might be the chosen one of God: perhaps he was the Messiah they were looking for. But he told them in these words that he was not: he was just a forerunner. He was the "voice crying in the wilderness," but he admitted that God was using him to prepare the way for Christ as He would come.

The one special day or season in the church calendar that seems to be most appreciated by the whole wide world is Christmas; and that is a very significant day. On that day God sent His only Son into the world to die for us. Perhaps it is fitting that the world should see in Christmas God's great word to them: "Come." But the day that is more important to a Christian, more important to a believer is the day of Pentecost. This is the day on which God sent His Holy Spirit into the hearts of believers. It emphasizes invisible things. The people of the world will not be impressed with something they cannot see, and this day deals with things that are personal and invisible. What happened at Pentecost took place inside the believer.

Pentecost implies that the resurrection of Jesus Christ is real, which is to say that it is based on the idea that the body of Jesus Christ actually rose from the dead. It follows then that whoever does not believe in the resurrection would not be much impressed with Pentecost. After all, if Christ Jesus did not rise from the dead, then there would be no meaning to the Day of Pentecost. Pentecost implies that heaven is real and that angels are real. It is sad but true that many people have no confidence in the actual reality of heaven and angels. It is surprising how many people feel they are thinking on a sound basis because so many other people seem to agree with them. They actually feel scarcely anybody believes in heaven. It is important to realize that Pentecost holds that Jesus of Nazareth is alive now. As a matter of fact Pentecost is based on that. It also holds that God the Father, God the Son, God the Holy Spirit, really come into a man to have fellowship with him and to bless him. This is what Pentecost means.

Pentecost is not just one of the Bible miracles, of which there are many. Pentecost promises real blessing, as a miracle that goes on and on. Man in himself is weak and he readily doubts. When the disciples were gathered together in the Upper Room, they were profoundly impressed. They had lived with Jesus of Nazareth and had been associated with Him for perhaps as much as three years. They had seen the events in the closing days of His life. They had been there on that tragic day when He was put on Calvary's Cross. They were there when He died. They knew about His body being put in the tomb. They hid out from the mob that was so angry with Him, but now they had· been told He was raised from the dead! Later, by the space of forty days He showed Himself alive by many infallible proofs.

One after another of the disciples had been shown convincingly that Jesus Christ was actually alive. You will remember Thomas who was not there the first time that Jesus came. When the disciples told him that they had seen the Lord, he could not believe it. He said he would not believe it unless he could put his fingers into His hands where the nails had been, and his hand into His side where the spear had been thrust. And you will recall that eight days later, while they were together and Thomas was there, that Jesus Himself appeared and spoke to Thomas. "Put your fingers here. Put your hand here." You will remember how Thomas fell at His feet and said, "My Lord and my God." And what happened to Thomas you can be sure in your own mind would have happened to any of them. The Lord Jesus spent forty days in showing them actually, really, literally that He was truly raised from the dead.

And then the disciples had seen Him ascend into heaven. All had been there on that day, when He was taken from their sight up into the heavens and a cloud received Him out of their sight. They had heard the message of the angels that said, "This same Jesus which is taken up from you into heaven, shall so come in like manner as ye have seen him go into heaven." Then they were told to go back to Jerusalem and wait for the promise of the Father.

The great truth that is set forth in Pentecost is that God will come to dwell among His people. The presence of God is to be a comfort. Human beings are face to face with many hard things, but the presence of God is to be an assurance. The believer can be led in his life by the very presence of God. The presence of God is to be a support that will strengthen the believer for every good thing.

The story of Pentecost is told in Acts 2.

> And when the day of Pentecost was fully come, they were all with one accord in one place. And suddenly there came a sound from heaven as of a rushing mighty wind, and it filled all the house where they were sitting. And there appeared unto them cloven tongues like as of fire, and it sat upon each of them. And they were all filled with the Holy Ghost, and began to speak with other tongues, as the Spirit gave them utterance. And there were dwelling at Jerusalem Jews, devout men, out of every nation under heaven. Now when this was noised abroad, the multitude came together, and were confounded, because that every man heard him speak in his own language (Acts 2:1-6).

Heaven is real. Out from the presence of God the Holy Spirit was sent. God wants fellowship with His children. He wants to be with them and He will come to dwell in the hearts of the believers. All of this had been promised in Old Testament times, and was revealed in the fulfillment of the Scripture.

When the Lord Jesus was here He gathered the members of His Body. He had gathered together His disciples into one place. They had yielded themselves to the Lord. The Lord had died for them. Everything had been done for them as it was written that it would be done. Now the disciples, in obedience to the Lord's command, were awaiting the promised Comforter. All was in readiness. A twelfth apostle had been appointed to take the place of Judas. Everything was just as it should be, and suddenly Pentecost occurred: the glory of God filled the believers with the presence of His Holy Spirit.

This could happen to anyone. Think of this! When a person believes, humbly, definitely believes in Christ, yields to Him, brings every part of his personal consciousness under the control of God, waits on God, is obedient in any and every way, this person can have the experience of suddenly being filled with the glorious consciousness that God has come to be with him. Thus he can have his own experience that in a sense is like Pentecost.

48.

Being Filled with the Spirit

Do you realize that no Christian is ever free to act or free to think as he pleases in himself?

The Christian is committed to obey the living Lord. "But be filled with the Spirit" (Ephesians 5:18). A more careful translation would be, "But be getting filled with the Spirit." The life of any Christian is featured by the fact that he is never alone. When he accepted Christ Jesus as Savior and was born again by the Word of God, the Christian received the Holy Spirit sent by God. The Spirit would take the things of Christ Jesus and show them to the believer, reminding the believer of what Christ has done and what He is doing and what He will do. This is the source of the life of a Christian.

But the believer's human nature continues to live in him, even after he has received the Holy Spirit, prompting desires which the Bible calls carnal and natural. Thus the Christian has a conflict in himself between flesh and spirit. He has his old nature and he has been given from God a new spiritual nature. He has been given the Holy Spirit of God. Paul writes in Galatians 5:16: "This I say then, Walk in the Spirit, and ye shall not fulfill the lust of the flesh."

It is as though a person were marching on the street, halfway between two bands: one band playing its marching music behind and the other band playing its marching music in front. If one of these has a fast temp, the other a slow one, the problem for the marcher is which of the two is he going to follow? If he marches in step with one, he will walk at a certain rate of speed, but if he listens to the other he will walk at a different rate of speed. The Christian is very much like that. He has the old man; he has the new man.

Paul had this in mind when he wrote "walk in the Spirit." The natural, which Paul calls the old nature, prompts me to do what I want to do. It promises me satisfaction and joy. The new man which comes from the Lord Jesus Christ and is the Holy Spirit, prompts me to see that fellowship with the living Lord is important and I will find my joy as I obey Him. These two natures are described by Paul:

> I am crucified with Christ: nevertheless I live; yet not I, but Christ liveth in me: and the life which I now live in the flesh I live by the faith of the Son of God, who loved me, and gave himself for me (Galatians 2:20).

The Apostle Paul was still Paul. He was still known as the man that they all had known and remembered; but he was also a new man in Christ Jesus, and this new Being in him was expecting to control him. When the Holy Spirit comes into the heart it is important to remember that He is God, and because He is God He expects to control me. I am a believer and I am committed to obey Him, but such obedience on my part will be imperfect. Even though I intend to obey Him and I want to obey Him, the truth of the matter is that I do not do it perfectly. I am not yielded 100 percent in this matter.

The Christian in his own experience has much unhappiness when he listens to the human part of him. There is much distress when in my spirit I feel I want to do the will of God but in my human nature I want to do what I would like to do. If I make my decisions as I please in my own self, that is living in the flesh, Paul would say that I am acting and living carnally. If I make my decisions as the Holy Spirit directs me, in the will of Christ, Paul would say I am living spiritually.

> For they that are after the flesh do mind the things of the flesh; but they that are after the Spirit the things of the Spirit (Romans 8:5).

I have in me both the flesh and the Spirit. Which one am I to follow? If I follow after my human ideas, I will be carnal; if I follow after my spiritual leading, I will be spiritual: I can do either one or the other. Paul goes on to say: "For to be carnally minded is death; but to be spiritually minded is life and peace." If I make my decisions as I want to as a human being, this is what Paul calls carnal. If I make my decisions as Christ Jesus wants me to as a member of His Body, as a spiritual being, that is spiritual. The degree to which I am yielded to the Spirit is never entirely perfect. I always have something of me in my own heart. It is true I can be more yielded or less yielded. I can be more than half yielded. I can be totally yielded at times. But generally my situation is such that I am not completely obedient to the Lord. The Holy Spirit may be strong in me and yet not be absolute in me. I may still be holding out some little thing away from His control. It may happen that when I face some crisis, some really big important thing, and I need to express myself in action, I find that I am helped to yield everything to the Lord and allow Him to take full control.

When I yield everything to Him and allow Him to take full control, I am having an experience that the Bible calls "filled with the Spirit." Paul exhorts the believers in Ephesus, "Be ye getting filled with the Spirit." The truth is that the Holy Spirit comes to the believer to take charge. For the Christian the process of becoming spiritual is a gradual growing development. He yields more and more and more to Him. A great writer one time in talking about these things pointed out that there were three phases in the experience of the Holy Spirit: the incoming of the Holy Spirit, the fullness of the Holy Spirit and the constant manifestation of the Holy Spirit. He pointed out that the secret of the incoming was union with Christ. The secret of the fullness was yielding to Christ. The secret of the constant manifestation of the Spirit in one's life results from abiding in Christ. Since the Holy Spirit wants to come into my heart, it's only necessary so far as I'm concerned that I open up and let Him in. I must let go whatever it is I am clinging to and let God have His way.

Being filled with the Spirit is much like having a room filled with sunlight. The thing to do is to lift the shade, move away the obstructions. I need to put away the things that are in the way. If I yield to Him, He will fill me to overflowing.

49.

Significance in the Scripture

Is it clear to you that God has given guidance to all men so that anybody, whosoever will, may come to Him to be saved?

> But continue thou in the things which thou hast learned and hast been assured of, knowing of whom thou hast learned them; and that from a child thou hast known the holy scriptures, which are able to make thee wise unto salvation through faith which is in Christ Jesus (II Timothy 3:14-15).

This is how Paul put it to Timothy: the Scriptures are able to make a person wise unto salvation. The wonderful truth in the gospel is that God wants to bless man. I remember as a lad I first heard that God loved man. I had never thought of that. I thought God was going to punish man. Man certainly needed it. I knew that God would punish me, I certainly needed it, and I was expecting it; but when people said that God loved me I was confused. If the people really believed God loved them, why then were they all so downhearted and so downcast while they were sitting in church? I had known them out in the street, on their farm, and they were not like that. But when they came to church they all seemed sad. If you have ever heard my testimony you will know I came to the conclusion that it was not true that God loved them, that there wasn't any God anyway; and that was one reason why they were so downhearted, because they did not have anything or anybody, in whom to put their trust. But I was wrong.

It is true that because of His personal integrity, God can bless only such as do His will. It is true that God is willing to bless anybody, and that He will bless everybody who comes to Him. It is also true that God calls all men unto Him. It must be remembered all

192

men will not come. Though salvation is prepared for all men, "whosoever will," you and I should keep in mind that whosoever will not, doesn't get it. That's all there is to it. We need to remember this and be careful not to leave the impression that God is some pale weak colorless Being, who will excuse everybody. Oh, no! God is God, and He is like a flame of fire! Those who have come to deal with God have found out that God is not going to accept sin or sinners or sinfulness.

But there is a way for a sinner to come to God. While it is true that God wants to bless man, and that He will bless any man who comes the way He has prepared, God can bless only such as do His will.

But how can man do the will of God if he does not know it? And how can God communicate His will to sinful man? God is in heaven. Man is on earth. How can God get His ideas and His will through to men on earth? The answer is by His Word. God will speak, man will hear and he will get the message. But the matter is not as simple as that sounds. God is in heaven; man is on earth. God is holy; man is sinful. God is infinite, unlimited; man is limited in time and in space. God is eternal; man is just for a few years. This creates the problem. How is Almighty God from heaven, holy, infinite and eternal, who has a plan that is eternal: how is He going to get the knowledge of that across to me, surrounded by the things of the world? It is written that God spake in times past unto the fathers by the prophets. He used these certain selected persons to convey His message to all people. God would speak to Moses, and Moses would speak to the people.

> Now all these things [referring to Old Testament events] happened unto them for examples: and they are written for our admonition, upon whom the ends of the world are come (I Corinthians 10:11).

> For whatsoever things were written aforetime were written for our learning, that we through patience and comfort of the scriptures might have hope (Romans 15:4).

The Word of God is eternal. The Word of God became incarnate in the flesh in Jesus of Nazareth, but the Word of God was also written in the Holy Scriptures. To communicate with human beings God revealed His will in certain human events that He carefully controlled and then had these recorded in the Holy Scriptures. To learn God's will we read the Bible.

In reading God's Word the content varies. The record of history is the history of the children of Israel. In this we discover general principles about God's way of dealing with men. The Bible also has in it much biography. We learn what happened to Jacob, Moses, Joseph, David, Daniel. And as we find out what happened to these persons, we are learning what could happen to us. There is also the "wisdom literature": the book of Job and the books of Proverbs and Ecclesiastes. In this wisdom literature, the reader will get ideas about living in the world. Then again there is a portion of the Scriptures that we call "poetical": speaking about the Song of Solomon, but mainly about the Psalms. The whole book of Psalms, one hundred and fifty of them, is called the Hymn Book of Israel. It is largely poetry and as we read the Psalms we learn how to say things. If I want to worship God I can read one of the Psalms and as I meditate in the presence of God I will find that some of the Psalms will say word for word just what my heart wants to say. Thus we learn the thought forms of the vocabulary of worship by reading the poetical books of the Bible.

There are also books in the Bible commonly called "prophecy." The Major Prophets are four: Isaiah, Jeremiah, Ezekiel and Daniel. The Minor Prophets are twelve. All the prophets are preachers that give exposition of God's will. If I want to find what God really meant by what He was doing with Israel, the prophets will tell me. As I come to the New Testament, I come to the "Gospels." As I read the Gospels I am seeing a demonstration of the truth of God. It is all set forth in the Person of Jesus of Nazareth. There is a manifestation: an open showing of God's plan in the world, to be seen in the birth, life, death, and resurrection of Jesus Christ.

When I read the book of "Acts," I find examples of Christian living, examples of Christian believing. After that I come to a group of books that we probably use more than any other part of the Bible called the "Epistles." These are letters written by the apostles and others to Christian people. In them I can get an understanding of the life of faith. Finally the last book in the Bible is the "Revelation of John." Here I will get assurance and comfort about God's plan in Christ Jesus. All aspects of the Bible reveal some truth about Jesus Christ. One needs to be familiar with the narratives because the truth is revealed in them as to what happened to Israel under God. Everything in the Bible points to Jesus Christ. He Himself said, "Search the Scriptures, for they are they which testify of me."

50.

The Scriptures and Spiritual Living

Do you realize that no human being could live a spiritual life, a Christian life, by himself in his own power even if he wanted to?

Abide in me, and I in you. As the branch cannot bear fruit of itself, except it abide in the vine; no more can ye, except ye abide in me. I am the vine, ye are the branches: He that abideth in me, and I in him, the same bringeth forth much fruit: for without me ye can do nothing. If a man abide not in me, he is cast forth as a branch, and is withered; and men gather them, and cast them into the fire, and they are burned. If ye abide in me, and my words abide in you, ye shall ask what ye will, and it shall be done unto you (John 15:4-7).

Believers are to have their spiritual life as from Jesus Christ. The Christian lives in God. Scripture in speaking about God says, "in whom we live and move and have our being." The Christian especially lives in relationship with the eternal truth of God.

When I became a Christian I did not put Jesus Christ on the cross. He already had died for me. What I did was to bring my soul in line with this overwhelming fact and receive it for myself. Men may know me in terms of my birth, residence, career, but actually as a Christian they do not yet know me, because as a Christian I am a child of God.

I have a Savior who is praying for me right now. He is in the presence of God interceding on my behalf. There is not a single thing that will happen to me, about which He is not aware; and not a single situation I will come into about which He is not concerned. Toward the end of His time upon earth, He told Peter: "Simon, Simon, behold, Satan hath desired to have you, that he may sift you as wheat: but I have prayed for thee, that thy faith fail not" (Luke 22:31-32). That same Lord is praying for me right now. I am disposed to look ahead, to make plans, even though I do not know what a day will bring forth. James warns about this:

> Go to now, ye that say, Today or tomorrow we will go into such a city, and continue there a year, and buy and sell, and get gain: whereas ye know not what shall be on the morrow. For what is your life? It is even a vapor, that appeareth for a little time, and then vanisheth away. For that ye ought to say, If the Lord will, we shall live, and do this, or that. But now ye rejoice in your boastings: all such rejoicing is evil (James 4:13-16).

If it is true that I am a child of God, and it is true that I have a Savior praying for me, and it is true that I do not know what a day will bring forth, then it will be important that I walk in His will. But how will I know what to do? "Commit thy way unto the Lord; trust also in him; and he shall bring it to pass" (Psalm 37:5). "Wherewithal shall a young man cleanse his way? By taking heed thereto according to thy word" (Psalm 119:9).

In many ways the course of spiritual events, the things that happen to me in my soul can be understood when I see the natural process. For instance I can remember "Whatsoever a man soweth that shall he also reap."

If a man sows to the Spirit, the things of the Lord, he shall of the Spirit reap life everlasting. That is true. If he sows to the flesh, he shall of the flesh reap corruption. That is true! But there is one basic difference. There is something more that the Christian needs to know.

In the natural world, where we live, law prevails: "Whatsoever a man soweth that shall he also reap." But in the spiritual world, where we live as Christians, as believers, grace is operative. God will do more for us than we can ask or think. Actually things will happen to us that we did not bring to pass. They will be given to us. The gift of God is eternal life through Jesus Christ our Lord, and for this reason, knowledge of the natural world is not enough.

We need to know how spiritual experience happens.

> Eye hath not seen, nor ear heard, neither have entered into the
> heart of man, the things which God hath prepared for them
> that love him. But God hath revealed them unto us by his
> Spirit: for the Spirit searcheth all things, yea, the deep things
> of God (I Corinthians 2:9-10).

The wisdom of this world is real and important, and it is very
impressive as far as it goes; but it doesn't go far enough. In living the
believer needs to have dealings with God. If I want to experience
spiritual living, I must grow in grace and in knowledge; and for this I
need to read and study and try to understand the Scriptures. I must
get acquainted with the Bible stories, learn to know the truth, the
record that is made of Bible men and Bible women. I must understand the worship procedures that are set forth in the Bible, meditate upon the miracles, the works of Jesus Christ, and remember the
present ministry of Jesus Christ in the presence of God. I must
honor the presence of the Holy Spirit in my heart and read the
Psalms to cultivate my vocabulary in praise. In this way, I may grow
in grace and in knowledge, and by His power improve my spiritual
living as a Christian.

51.

The Use of Scripture in Personal Experience

Can you understand why Bible reading and Bible study are so helpful to a Christian as he lives his daily life?

All scripture is given by inspiration of God, and is profitable for doctrine, for reproof, for correction, for instruction in righteousness: that the man of God may be perfect, throughly furnished unto all good works (II Timothy 3:16-17).

When Paul says that "the man of God may be perfect" he has in mind that the man of God should be full-grown, should be mature, should be bearing fruit, as an apple tree when the apples begin to appear on it: that he may come through to full grown Christian experience. "Throughly furnished:" that word "throughly" is also well translated "thoroughly" furnished unto all good works. Did you notice that the Scriptures were not given so that this man might be happy? They were given to the man of God that man might be equipped unto all good work. The whole purpose of the gospel is that the individual believer may be useful in the will of God, useful in God's plan.

Bible reading is often recommended as a beneficial exercise: as if there were some sort of magic about it. The idea seems to be that if I read one verse I will be blessed; if I read three verses I will be blessed three times as much. There is an element of possibility in that, but that is not really the way to put it. And again Bible study is often promoted by some that they might indoctrinate others with a certain view of the gospel in mind. But there are more important reasons for reading the Bible.

The life of a Christian is different from the life of any natural

199

person. The natural person sees only the immediate meaning of things, what's here and now; but the spiritual person, the person who has been born again and is a child of God, sees also the eternal meanings, the things that last forever. The Bible makes this possible.

Have you ever wondered about what actually happens when you plant a seed in the ground? I'm sure we are all familiar with the seed of the oak tree, an acorn. In the acorn is contained all the oakness of the oak tree. The soil will not make any difference. The acorn will always produce an oak in any situation. And so it is with anyone who lives according to the Scriptures.

Sometimes the idea is advanced that if conditions were better, people would be better. This is true only in a very limited way. That acorn that fell into the ground on that hillside produced an oak tree. If an apple seed had fallen into that same ground right beside it, there could have been an apple tree. If anyone had planted a seed of a flower, such as a rose, in the ground right there, there could have been a rose bush. In other words, the ground did not make the difference in the kind of plant. Of course, if the ground was fertile and well watered, the oak tree would grow fast and large. The soil does make a difference in the experience, but it does not change the nature of the plant.

The meaning of this discussion is that the Bible, the Word of God, is the seed, and as people get to know and believe the Bible, they will become Christians. This will be true regardless of whether the home is rich or poor. This young man may be a strong athlete, but as he reads the Bible and learns that Christ Jesus is his Savior he can become a Christian. That person over there may be a cripple, so that he walks with crutches, but as he reads the Bible and finds that Christ Jesus is his Savior he can become a Christian. The Bible, the Word of God, is the seed. It enters into the heart and produces a child of God.

The more I read, study and understand the Bible, the more I will grow as a child of God into the likeness of the Son of God. I will actually become more and more like Him.

The living of any Christian is grounded in his faith, according to the way he believes. Faith needs to be nurtured, that it may grow. "Faith cometh by hearing and hearing by the Word of God."

The Bible can also be thought of as the Bread of Life. When Moses was leading the children of Israel in the desert they were fed with manna, which was bread from heaven. The children of Israel were in the desert; when the manna appeared each morning they were to collect it. The manna was to be collected in the early morning before the sun rose, so that it would not melt away. This teaches us that the Scriptures should be read before trouble comes. Before the sun rises with its heat.

If I wait until I am in trouble and then start reading the Bible I may falter. If I would read the Bible first, then when trouble comes the Bible will sustain me.

There was more to be learned in this incident. The children of Israel were not to collect manna for tomorrow, for the next day. If they collected more manna than they could use on that day, it would spoil. They had to have each day's supply, except of course on the Sabbath Day. They were permitted on the day before the Sabbath to collect twice as much. This presents good guidance for all Christians. Bible reading must be done regularly, and read before having trouble. I must read until I have enough for that day. Bible reading Christians are always strong in faith.

This is why missionaries teach the people to read. When missionaries go out to the foreign field and tell the natives about the Lord Jesus Christ, they tell what is true, and the native comes to understand that in the sight of God he is a sinner, which is true. Then he learns that Christ Jesus is the Son of God who came to die for sinners and that is true. Then he is told that if he receives Christ Jesus as his Savior he will become a child of God and will be saved: all that is true. Then why would he need to read the Bible? Why is the missionary so anxious that this person should have the Bible in his hand? Why should he labor to translate the Bible into the language of the natives, and then teach the natives to read it? Because reading the Bible and reading the Bible and reading the Bible is all helpful for their spiritual life and growth.

This is why such organizations as the Pocket Testament League carry on their work. They aim to get the Bible into the pocket of people. This is why the Gideons distribute the Bible. This is why they put them in hotel rooms. They want to put them there where men can read them. This is why the American Bible Society arranges to have Bibles printed in so many different languages. They want the people to know the Bible. And this is why the Wycliffe Bible translators go out and do their work. They want to translate the Bible. Why? Because the reading of the Bible is essential to the spiritual experience of the people.

As you live and move, you should read over and over again, read with an open mind, and remember when you're reading it was written for you. It was not written for the theologians, or for the scholars. The Bible was written for you. You should open the Bible and read it as if it were talking to you; and then pray. On the basis of what you read, pray with a willing spirit, and then reach conclusions for yourself for that day. Bible reading Christians are always blessed of the Lord.

52.

Renewal and Revival

Do you think it is possible to have a change of heart in your feelings about anybody?

> And be not conformed to this world: but be ye transformed by the renewing of your mind (Romans 12:2).

> And be renewed in the spirit of your mind (Ephesians 4:23).

Renewal and revival are two words commonly used by people in referring to Christian experience. They are often used interchangeably as if they had the same meaning, but this is missing an important truth. Renewal might well refer to what happens in regeneration, when a person is born again. Experiencing the new birth is not a matter of having been a failure in the natural being and then becoming a success still in the natural. Being born again is not a project to improve the person by removing undesirable things and strengthening the desirable so as to improve the whole image of that person. Paul writes:

> Therefore if any man be in Christ, he is a new creature: old things are passed away; behold, all things are become new (II Corinthians 5:17).

Being born again is not only a new birth, but it is a different birth. Being born again is a case of a person once born in nature, being born again in spirit.

Renewal thus is a person born once in nature, and then having a new birth in spirit. Take Tom Smith, born of his parents he is a child of the flesh. He starts out as a baby in nature with no awareness of God. As a natural person there is no awareness of other people or respect for authority. There is no charity for the poor and no sense of forgiveness. In the natural world it's "whatsoever a man soweth that shall he also reap."

When Tom Smith hears the gospel of Jesus Christ, and comes to believe that God sent His Son to die for him, something happens to him. The Bible says he is born again, he has experienced a new birth and now is a child of God, being born of the Spirit. He now becomes inwardly aware of God. He becomes aware of God, heaven, judgment, the grace of God and the forgiveness of sin. Because of the grace of God given to him, Tom Smith actually wants to be found well pleasing. He has consideration for other people. He actually has charity for the poor, and he knows about the forgiveness of sin. Now this is what is meant by renewal and that can happen to anybody that will believe in the Lord Jesus Christ.

Coming to faith, accepting Christ, being forgiven, is often a glowing experience; but faith is not constant. Faith can wane, and weaken. It is written that the living Lord Jesus Christ sent this message to the church at Ephesus:

> Nevertheless I have somewhat against thee, because thou hast left thy first love. Remember therefore from whence thou art fallen, and repent, and do the first works (Revelation 2:4-5).

This was spoken by the Lord Jesus to a very good congregation, a very good church. Again in the next chapter this message was sent to the church at Sardis.

> Thou hast a name that thou livest, and art dead. Be watchful, and strengthen the things which remain, that are ready to die (Revelation 3:1-2).

Here is a church of which the Lord says: "though people say about you that you are alive, actually you are dead."

When faith becomes weak the awareness of God dims. So consideration for others can become less. So charity for the poor can disappear. So forgiveness can be forgotten, and when I forget about my forgiveness I feel guilty and begin to hold grudges against other people. This describes the experience of a person whose faith has weakened and who has become less in the Lord than he could be.

I must remember that unless I feed my faith, my faith will become weaker. I may know perfectly well that God is real, yet I can live as if there were no God. I may know right well that the things of heaven are true, yet I can be so involved in the things of this world that I forget that I have a home in heaven. Now what can I do about this? I can worship God. I can go to the public worship of God. I can go to a Bible class, and to prayer meeting. I can be very sure that if I will start looking into the presence of God, things will come back to life in me. I need to read and study the Bible. I need to join with other people who read and study the Bible. I need to pray and join praying people as they pray. And then I need to witness. I need to identify myself as a person that does believe, and show in my deeds, in what I do, that it is real to me. Among other things I need to make use of my money. I can tithe! If I feel things dull spiritually, and I begin to wonder whether I am really as close to the Lord as I ought to be, I can help by doubling what I am already giving. If I will do that, I will soon see the blessing that will come to me. If I will honor the Lord's Day, give to missions and give to the poor, this will be revival in me.

53.

Revivals during the Judges

If a man realized he was neglecting God, would he have to stay like that? How could he change?

Another important aspect of Christian experience is indicated by the word "revival." A believer's faith may weaken but it can be restored. This was illustrated early in the life of Israel, at the time of the Judges. The children of Israel had developed as a nation in the land of Egypt. When Jacob and his sons came down to Egypt while Joseph was there, there were some seventy souls altogether. Four hundred years later, when they were leaving that country, they had become thousands in number. They came out of the land of Egypt, traveled across the desert, which took them forty years. They then came into the land of Canaan as they were led by Joshua. Joshua guided them in their conquest of the country and when he died left them with some very definite instructions how to proceed to complete their conquest.

Following the time of Joshua, there was a period of four hundred years in the history of Israel when their public life was relatively uncontrolled. Each tribe lived pretty much as it saw fit. It is true they united around the worship of God. They had the same promise, the covenant of Abraham, and they had the same guidance, the law of Moses. They all followed the same practices, the worship of God through the procedures of the sons of Aaron, the Levites, the Levitical priesthood.

As a people the Israelites were banded together largely because of their faith in God. They learned that blessedness came as they exercised faith in God and were obedient.

The Bible teaches me now that blessedness, the favor of God in my daily life, comes as I believe in God. It is according to my faith, that it will be unto me. When I have more faith I am more inclined to obedience. And when there is more obedience, there will be more blessing. But it is also true that if there is less faith there will be less obedience, and when there is less obedience there will be less blessing.

This was illustrated in the time of Israel, and is recorded in the Book of Judges. The following quotation may be taken as a summary of what happened in Israel over the space of four hundred years.

> And when Joshua had let the people go, the children of Israel went every man unto his inheritance to possess the land. And the people served the Lord all the days of Joshua, and all the days of the elders that outlived Joshua, who had seen all the great works of the Lord, that he did for Israel. And Joshua the son of Nun, the servant of the Lord, died, being a hundred and ten years old. And they buried him in the border of his inheritance in Timnathheres, in the mount of Ephraim, on the north side of the hill Gaash. And also all that generation were gathered unto their fathers: and there arose another generation after them, which knew not the Lord, nor yet the works which he had done for Israel (Judges 2:6-10).

When the Bible uses the word "know" in this fashion, "which knew not the Lord," it means not so much that they had never heard of Him, as that they did not appreciate Him, they did not honor Him, they did not actually "know" who God really was, so far as they were concerned. So they did not "know" the Lord: they did not appreciate the Lord nor yet the works that He had done for Israel. In this they were like children growing up in a Christian home. They may have heard about God, Jesus Christ, and about the gospel, and taken these for granted. It may never have dawned on them that they were to live by these truths. That is the way it was with Israel.

"And the children of Israel did evil in the sight of the Lord, and served Baalim" (Judges 2:11). The word "Baalim" refers to the gods of the heathen, who were the gods of power. In other words, Israel did evil in the sight of the Lord by going after the things that made for strength and for power in natural ways so that they could get what they wanted.

> And they forsook the Lord God of their fathers, which brought them out of the land of Egypt, and followed other gods, of the gods of the people that were round about them, and bowed themselves unto them, and provoked the Lord to anger (Judges 2:12).

Today this would mean to say they had the Bible, they had the Gospel, they went to church, but their interest was in other things. "And they forsook the Lord, and served Baal and Ashtaroth." Baal was the god of power and Ashtaroth was the goddess of pleasure. Today this would mean money and pleasure. God would not tolerate such conduct. "And the anger of the Lord was hot against Israel." As we may have committed our children to God and have tried to teach them truth about the gospel and then their hearts and minds become filled with other things, God is not pleased. If they think only of what is going on downtown, when they have heard about God in the church, so that now they are interested solely in what goes on in the stadium, they are interested in what goes on in popular activities — God notices that: it does not please Him.

The anger of the Lord was hot against Israel, and he delivered them into the hands of the spoilers that spoiled them" (Judges 2:14). The word "spoiled" means "robbed." In other words God withdrew His favor, and when He did these people began to lose. Other people took things away from them.

> He sold them into the hands of their enemies round about, so that they could not any longer stand before their enemies (Judges 2:14).

This helps us to understand what happens when Christians stop reading the Bible, when they stop committing themselves to God in prayer. Then they may get all tangled up with psychology and social problems and such natural considerations. They may be trying to do something for themselves, but they are leaving God out of their thinking.

Whithersoever they went out, the hand of the Lord was against them for evil, as the Lord had said, and as the Lord had sworn unto them: and they were greatly distressed (Judges 2:15).

How would such distress be seen today? When there is no obedience; when the parents and young people do not have any standards; when they do not think for one moment about God. As this happens to God's own people, He withdraws His favor. When He withdraws His favor, then God's people will lose out. Many blessings which resulted from faith in God will fall away.

Nevertheless the Lord raised up judges, which delivered them out of the hand of those that spoiled them (Judges 2:16).

Those judges were similar to revival preachers we know today. But even this ministry was not able to turn them from their unbelieving ways.

And yet they would not hearken unto their judges, but they went a whoring after other gods, and bowed themselves unto them: they turned quickly out of the way which their fathers walked in, obeying the commandments of the Lord; but they did not so. And when the Lord raised them up judges, then the Lord was with the judge, and delivered them out of the hand of their enemies all the days of the judge: for it repented the Lord because of their groanings by reason of them that oppressed them and vexed them (Judges 2:17-18).

While these preachers preached, and the people listened and obeyed, God was gracious to them. He would hear their cry and turn to them. But alas, "And it came to pass, when the judge was dead," when the revival preacher was gone, "that they returned, and corrupted themselves more than their fathers, in following other gods to serve them, and to bow down unto them; they ceased not from their own doings, nor from their stubborn way." It is no wonder that it is written in the rest of this chapter, "And the anger of the Lord was hot against Israel; and he said, Because that this people hath transgressed my covenant which I commanded their fathers, and have not hearkened unto my voice; I also will not henceforth drive out any from before them of the nations which Joshua left when he died" (Judges 2:20-21). Here again is an indication of God's way of doing things which helps us to understand why even in our time, God allows the existence of natural elements and factors to turn His people away from Him.

54.

Revival under Samuel

If a person realized his own faith was not what it used to be, or what it should be, are there any steps he could take to correct this condition?

In learning about living by faith, we find that faith is the basis of all that ever happens in the life of a Christian. Matters of faith are hard to grasp, because they deal with the invisible. For this reason we need to seek examples in Scripture. By the good providence of God we have a complete account of a revival in the life of Israel, reported in I Samuel 7:2. The account begins with this statement: "And it came to pass, while the ark abode in Kirjath-jearim, that the time was long." This shows that the ark was not where it should have been. It should have been in the Tabernacle, the sanctuary of God, and it was not there. There is an amazing fitness in this statement to our situation today. There seems to be no doubt that with us the Bible is not in its right place. Even when we have the Book on the pulpit in the front of the Sanctuary, you can ask yourself, How much is the Book actually used by the preacher as he preaches and teaches whatever message he is setting forth?

The report goes on to note that while the ark was not in its right place "the time was long; for it was twenty years; and all the house of Israel lamented after the Lord." When things aren't right, when the Bible is not in its right place, the church is not blessed. Those people are not blessed in the Lord. There is no joy and no radiance. In this case of Israel, the people lamented for twenty years. The report simply states "the time was long." Have you ever had such a feeling? In your congregation, has it been a long time since there has been real blessing? In Israel the people lamented: they felt badly.

Under these circumstances, with their longing and wishing for something better, Samuel came to them:

> And Samuel spake unto all the house of Israel, saying, If ye do return unto the Lord with all your hearts, then put away the strange gods and Ashtaroth from among you, and prepare your hearts unto the Lord, and serve him only: and he will deliver you out of the hand of the Philistines (I Samuel 7:3).

This is preaching. This is saying to the people: "Do you feel badly? Do you wish things were better? Do you really with all your hearts actually want the blessing of God? Then put away the strange gods, put away the ideas that are popular, put away the things that you've picked up from the culture of the day and from the things of this world. Put away your popular ideas of pleasure from among you. Prepare your hearts unto the Lord. Bring yourself face to face with God. Take the Ten Commandments and let them speak to you. Face them as they are. Serve Him only, and He will deliver you out of the hands of the Philistines." Do you recognize that kind of preaching? Do you know what that man is saying? Repent! Draw nigh to God! Do you really mean it? Do you really want some blessing? Do you really want it to be better than it is? Are you sick and tired of this going on and on and on with no blessing? Do you really want to turn to God? Then repent!

"Then the children of Israel did put away Baalim and Ashtaroth, and served the Lord only" (I Samuel 7:4). They deliberately undertook to come to God. They began to read their Bibles. They began to go to church. They began to pray. They really wanted to seek the Lord. But this was not all that happened. That was just the start of it. "And Samuel said, Gather all Israel to Mizpeh, and I will pray for you unto the Lord" (I Samuel 7:5). Do you really want God's blessing? You have made a start. You have actually put away popular ideas and pleasure ideas out of your mind? You really have turned yourself to God! This was the right way to do it!

Samuel then led them into special spiritual emphasis. He planned special services. He brought all Israel together to pray. "And they gathered together to Mizpeh, and drew water, and poured it out before the Lord" (I Samuel 7:6). This was a custom that those people practiced that went along with confession of sin. They poured out their hearts before God. They admitted the way things actually were "and fasted on that day." Here is repentance with confession of sin and fasting. "We have sinned against the Lord." This acknowledgment of sin is very basic in deepening spiritual experience. "And Samuel judged the children of Israel in Mizpeh" (I Samuel 7:6). When the report reads that he judged them, this means he brought the Scriptures to bear upon them. He preached the Bible to them, and he showed them how barren their lives were. They listened honestly and studied the Word of God under the leadership of Samuel as earnest sincere dedicated people.

> And when the Philistines heard that the children of Israel were gathered together to Mizpeh, the lords of the Philistines went up against Israel. And when the children of Israel heard it, they were afraid of the Philistines (I Samuel 7:7).

What happened here was that Israel met opposition. And this will be universally true! When anybody really wants to turn to God, and really wants to become spiritual, and become godly, there will be opposition.

> And the children of Israel said to Samuel, Cease not to cry unto the Lord our God for us, that he will save us out of the hand of the Philistines (I Samuel 7:8).

These people were crying out to Samuel: "We do have this trouble, we face this opposition, but we do believe in God. Pray for us." "And Samuel took a sucking lamb, and offered it for a burnt offering wholly unto the Lord." (I Samuel 7:9).

Whenever the Old Testament speaks of a burnt offering, the meaning is consecration: a complete yielding to God. Samuel called these people to come and yield themselves totally and entirely to God, which they did. "And Samuel cried unto the Lord for Israel; and the Lord heard him." Here we see the call to consecration and intercessory prayer. It is wonderful to read that the tide of battle was turned against the Philistines and Israel was given a great victory.

"Then Samuel took a stone, and set it between Mizpeh and Shen, and called the name of it Ebenezer, saying, Hitherto hath the Lord helped us" (I Samuel 7:12). This was praise to God for the victory. This is the classic pattern of revival.

This will be true for any individual person, and it will be true for any congregation. Here is the pattern. It starts out with hunger and thirst for blessing. This is essential. But don't give up! If you haven't been blessed, ask. If you are not being blessed, pray: hunger and thirst! That brought on preaching. They called on a man to preach, and you can be confident there will always be preachers ready to come. This preacher, Samuel, preached a very simple message: Get right with God. Bring yourself into the presence of God. This they did with repentance and fasting and confession. They really sought God. That took some time and this will always be involved in any total overall revival. It never will be an afternoon affair. It will go on and on and on and that will arouse opposition. But when this opposition came, they did not quit. They prayed and they called on Samuel: "Pray for us." And Samuel called on them to dedicate themselves, to consecrate themselves to God, put themselves one hundred percent into this matter. Then in intercessory prayer, Samuel cried to Almighty God for blessing and God gave them the victory. Now Samuel led them all in praise. We should never stop till we thank God for the whole victory.

As Christian people, there will be times when things are not right with us. When we are really aching and being bothered, let us remember that "hungering and thirsting" are important. Then listen to the preaching. Let that preaching be straight from the Bible. It will lead believers to repentance and to confession. Then there will be opposition. Face it down. Do not quit. You will not have to face it in your own strength: call on God. Ask people to help you. Join in prayer. "Where two or three are gathered together in prayer there am I in the midst of them." You may expect from God a great victory. Then you can praise God for it. That is the pattern of revival.

55.

Revival under Hezekiah

(I)

If a congregation of Christians such as a church were suffering from inadequate, poor spiritual practices or procedures, is there anything that could be done about it?

We can learn much about spiritual experience by noting what happened in Israel in the Old Testament. Those things were written for our learning: they happened to them for examples, and they're written for us that we might learn. Just now we are studying revival, when the faith and the life of God's people are restored to a strong healthy condition. The fact is that faith can become weak. Understanding may become confused, and assurance may be lacking. Such a condition is never a sudden happening. It would not occur overnight. It would be the consequence of prolonged neglect and tolerance of evil. Such a situation confronted King Hezekiah when he came to the throne. We read about this both in the books of II Kings and II Chronicles. A full report of this event is found in II Chronicles 28-29.

Hezekiah was twenty-five years of age when he came to the throne of Judah following his father, who had been an evil man. His father's name was Ahaz and he is one of the few kings of Judah who was actually a wicked man, and brought upon himself and the nation the judgment of God:

> For the Lord brought Judah low because of Ahaz king of Israel; for he made Judah naked, and transgressed sore against the Lord (II Chronicles 28:19).

This is a solemn warning that a congregation today can be brought low when the minister conducts himself in such a way that the people become spiritually naked, and the minister himself actually transgresses against the Lord in the things that he does. So often people feel this refers only to immorality, but that is not always the case. A minister is not doing right, if he isn't preaching God's Word. If a man is in the ministry and does not teach his people what is in the Bible he has done wrong. Also, if a man is in the pulpit and talks about people getting right with God while he does not bring to their minds that they are sinners and that they need to be saved, he is doing wrong. Just so if he teaches about coming to God and having fellowship with God while making you think that you can come into the presence of God to have the blessing of God without ever bringing in the idea of repentance and sin, he is wrong. Such a man transgresses sorely against the Lord. A minister like that will bring his congregation low. This has been done in the time of Ahaz, king of Israel.

When Hezekiah, his son, strangely enough the righteous son of a wicked father, came to the throne he set out to do right.

> And he did that which was right in the sight of the Lord, according to all that David his father had done. He in the first year of his reign, in the first month, opened the doors of the house of the Lord, and repaired them (II Chronicles 29:2-3).

He encouraged people to come into the presence of God. He found the gates of the temple in a state of neglect and repaired them. I could ask myself what do I have to repair? It will be something that has been neglected. If a congregation has been so lax that the impression has been given that anybody can come to God anyway, that it does not really matter how one comes to God, then the whole situation is suffering from neglect. It is as if someone had knocked the door off of the hinges.

When Hezekiah came to the throne and saw the neglected condition of the temple, the first thing he did was to fix up the doors. This signified something to anyone coming in. It meant that when a soul would come in, the door would be shut behind him, and he would be shut away from things. The unhappy, unblessed condition of Israel was the result of their neglect of the worship of God.

God is worshipped at the house of God. When this young man Hezekiah took over the first thing he did was go to the house of God and look at the evidence of carelessness. There had been neglect about the matter of coming into the presence of God. So the first thing he did was to correct that: he opened the doors and repaired them.

"And he brought in the priests and the Levites." The priests were the men who conducted the routine worship services and the Levites were the teachers. They were the people who taught the people to worship God, who did what Ezra did later in teaching them the Word of God. So he brought in the worship leaders, "and gathered them together into the east street."

Hezekiah showed his intelligence by calling in his officers first of all. He called in his leaders. It is plain to see that if they are not right nothing is going to happen in that congregation. Calling in his officers to listen to him the young king, Hezekiah, said: "Hear me, ye Levites, sanctify now yourselves." This simply means "Get right with God!"

> Sanctify now yourselves, and sanctify the house of the Lord God of your fathers, and carry forth the filthiness out of the holy place (II Chronicles 29:5).

"Filthiness" probably referred to debris which would have gathered in the building that had been casually neglected over a long period of time. Do you realize that when he told those men "Sanctify yourselves," he simply meant "Clean yourselves up. Get right with God and get the house of God clean by carrying out the filthiness from the holy place."

Continuing, he went on to say:

> My sons, be not now negligent: for the Lord hath chosen you to stand before him, to serve him, and that ye should minister unto him, and burn incense (II Chronicles 29:11).

He is calling to the attention of these officers, these leaders: "You've got a responsibility. You've been put in a certain place and now get out and show it. You're supposed to be acceptable before God. You have the privilege of serving God personally as an example to others."

Then the Levites arose.

> And they gathered their brethren, and sanctified themselves, and came, according to the commandment of the king, by the words of the Lord, to cleanse the house of the Lord. And the priests went into the inner part of the house of the Lord, to cleanse it, and brought out all the uncleanness that they found in the temple (II Chronicles 29:15-16).

The Levites took the debris and carried it out to the brook Kidron. They threw it out and put it away. Thus these men obeyed the word of the king.

> Then Hezekiah the king rose early, and gathered the rulers of the city, and went up to the house of the Lord (II Chronicles 29:20).

There they made an offering. They brought in a sin offering, which means that they confessed their sins.

> For the king commanded that the burnt offering and the sin offering should be made for all Israel (II Chronicles 29:24).

So they repented, confessed their sins and got right with God.

> And he set the Levites in the house of the Lord with cymbals, with psalteries, and with harps. . . . And the Levites stood with the instruments of David, and the priests with the trumpets. And Hezekiah commanded to offer the burnt offering upon the altar. And when the burnt offering began, the song of the Lord began also with the trumpets, and with the instruments. . . . And all the congregation worshiped, and the singers sang, and the trumpeters sounded: and all this continued until the burnt offering was finished (II Chronicles 29:25-28).

Thus they sang praises unto the Lord. The people were so deeply moved that when they were asked to bring in sacrifices and thank offerings, the response was more than they expected. They had so many animals brought in for sacrifices there were not enough priests to take care of them. Because the priests were too few the Levites helped them. The record is "the Levites were more upright in heart to sanctify themselves than the priests." There were more of the Bible teachers ready to do the Word of God, the will of God, than those who carried on the routine services of the congregation.

So the service of the house of the Lord was set in order. And Hezekiah rejoiced, and all the people, that God had prepared the people: for the thing was done suddenly (II Chronicles 29:35-36).

It wasn't dragged out. They did everything promptly. The people rejoiced. This was a great event in the life of Israel. It is very important to note that revival began with the preachers, teachers and officers.

56.

Revival under Hezekiah

(II)

Can you understand how the people in any congregation will be blessed after the leaders get right with God?

Now when Ezra had prayed, and when he had confessed, weeping and casting himself down before the house of God, there assembled unto him out of Israel a very great congregation of men and women and children: for the people wept very sore (Ezra 10:1).

The account in Ezra shows how a leader can affect the people. Ezra the leader prayed, confessed, wept and cast himself down before the Lord. A multitude of the people did as he did in coming to God.

And Shechaniah the son of Jehiel, one of the sons of Elam, answered and said unto Ezra, We have trespassed against our God, and have taken strange wives of the people of the land: yet now there is hope in Israel concerning this thing. Now therefore let us make a covenant with our God to put away all the wives, and such as are born of them, according to the counsel of my lord, and of those that tremble at the commandment of our God; and let it be done according to the law. Arise; for this matter belongeth unto thee: we also will be with thee: be of good courage, and do it (Ezra 10:2-4).

Here a layman rose up and said to his preacher: "You can do something about this. Yes, we've done wrong, but God is God and He will hear us. Arise, this matter belongs to you. We also will be with thee. Be of good courage and do it." Ezra did, and the people were blessed.

Have you ever wondered what would happen in any church if the preacher and his officers "got religion?" You can be sure of one result: the people would be blessed. Earlier Hezekiah brought his ministers to God. You will remember when this young man, Hezekiah, took over in the first year of his reign: he went straight to the House of God because that was the center of all their problems. He found the results of neglect which he repaired. He called in the priests and Levites and told them, "Get right with God." There was revival under Hezekiah's leadership.

"Hezekiah sent to all Israel and Judah, and wrote letters also to Ephraim and Manasseh, (Hezekiah began a publicity campaign) that they should come to the house of the Lord at Jerusalem, to keep the passover unto the Lord God of Israel" (II Chronicles 30:1). He sent word to all the people who professed to believe and called them to return to God. When mention is made about keeping the passover, you will remember the passover was the ceremony, the feast, that commemorated the passover in Egypt. That in turn will remind you that because of the shed blood put on the door posts, the angel of death passed over the people who had obeyed God. (The blessed truth is God forgives sin for Christ's sake. Christ is our Passover, slain for us.)

Although at that time Israel was divided into two nations, the northern with ten tribes, called Israel, and the southern with two tribes called Judah, Hezekiah's call was sent out to all, ignoring the division in the nation. (Today such a call would go out to all Christians everywhere without regard to denomination.)

. . . For they had not done it of a long time in such sort as it was written. So the posts went with the letters from the king and his princes throughout all Israel and Judah, and according to the commandment of the king, saying, Ye children of Israel, turn again unto the Lord God of Abraham, Isaac, and Israel, and he will return to the remnant of you, that are escaped out of the hand of the kings of Assyria. And be not ye like your fathers, and like your brethren, which trespassed against the Lord God of their fathers, who therefore gave them up to desolation, as ye see. Now be ye not stiffnecked, 'as your fathers were, but yield yourselves unto the Lord, and enter into his sanctuary, which he hath sanctified for ever: and serve the Lord your God, that the fierceness of his wrath may turn away from you. For if ye turn again unto the Lord, your brethren and your children shall find compassion before them that lead them captive, so that they shall come again into this land: for the Lord your God is gracious and merciful, and will not turn away his face from you, if ye return unto him (II Chronicles 30:5-9).

This was the gracious promise that was sent out everywhere. Regardless of how they had lived, or what they had done, they were called to turn to God and He would keep them. But this gracious promise was ignored. "So the posts passed from city to city through the country of Ephraim and Manasseh even unto Zebulun: but they laughed them to scorn, and mocked them" (II Chronicles 30:10). When this invitation went out there were some people that ignored the invitation and scorned it. Certainly they were promised, "If you will turn to God He will bless you." But their response was, "Well, who cares?"

"Nevertheless divers of Asher and Manasseh and of Zebulun humbled themselves, and came to Jerusalem. Also in Judah the hand of God was to give them one heart to do the commandment of the king and of the princes, by the word of the Lord" (II Chronicles 30:11-12). So the call that was sent out was ignored and scorned by some, and heeded in humility by others.

Some of them who were called and wanted to come were not fully prepared. They had not thought about it, and were not ready for it. They had not sanctified themselves. They were still doing things that were not as they ought to be. "But Hezekiah prayed for them, saying, The good Lord pardon every one that prepareth his heart to seek God, . . . though he be not cleansed according to the purification of the sanctuary. And the Lord hearkened to Hezekiah, and healed the people" (II Chronicles 30:18-20).

This was followed by great rejoicing. "The children of Israel that were present at Jerusalem, kept the feast of unleavened bread seven days with great gladness: and the Levites and the priests praised the Lord day by day, singing with loud instruments unto the Lord. And Hezekiah spake comfortably unto all the Levites that taught the good knowledge of the Lord" (II Chronicles 30:21-22). When it says he "spake comfortably" it means he spoke, comforting them, promising them the goodness of God. The people did eat of the sacrifices, they offered peace offerings and were making confession. The whole congregation had such joy they wanted it prolonged. "The whole assembly took counsel to keep other seven days" (II Chronicles 30:23). Have you ever heard of protracted meetings? Have you ever been present in a revival series for a week when the people were so blessed they continued for another week? That is what these people did.

The whole assembly took counsel to keep other seven days and they kept other seven days with gladness. "For Hezekiah king of Judah did give to the congregation a thousand bullocks and seven thousand sheep; and the princes gave to the congregation a thousand bullocks and ten thousand sheep: and a great number of priests sanctified themselves" (II Chronicles 30:24).

Hezekiah started out by calling in the officers. He got them altogether and started working with them: the Levites, the teachers of the Scriptures, sanctified themselves more quickly. The priests did not respond so quickly, but after the meeting had gone on, with the people turning to God, and a large company of people seeking God and having asked for another seven days, lo and behold! a great number of the priests sanctified themselves. The blessing had finally come even to the preachers, who now committed themselves to God.

"And all the congregation of Judah, with the priests and the Levites, and all the congregation that came out of Israel, and the strangers that came out of the land of Israel, and that dwelt in Judah, rejoiced. So there was great joy in Jerusalem: for since the time of Solomon the son of David king of Israel there was not the like in Jerusalem" (II Chronicles 30:25-26). This always happens when people get right with God. Great joy! And here is this final result:

Then the priests the Levites arose and blessed the people: and their voice was heard, and their prayer came up to his holy dwelling place, even unto heaven (II Chronicles 30:27).

Now the preachers could pray with power. The elders and the deacons could actually pray with power because the people had turned to God, with great joy and gladness. All of these things taken together give us a picture of revival among the people of God.

57.
Revival in the Church Today

If a person's spiritual life shows no signs of being alive, does it mean that such a person is spiritually hopeless?

"I know thy works, that thou hast a name that thou livest, and art dead. Be watchful, and strengthen the things which remain, that are ready to die" (Revelation 3:1-2). This was written for us. Because there is a special promise, "Blessed is he that readeth, and they that hear the words of this prophecy, and keep those things which are written therein" (Revelation 1:3), we take this to heart. This word was spoken by Jesus Christ Himself from glory, as He looked out upon a group of Christian people and said, "I know thy works, that thou hast a name that thou livest, and art dead" (Revelation 3:1). This would mean a message today to a congregation in a church: "You have the name of being Christians: you are supposed to be; your forefathers were. You have that tradition, but actually in yourselves you are doing nothing. The fact is you are dead." The Scripture goes on to record the Word of the Living Lord: "Be watchful, and strengthen the things which remain, that are ready to die" (Revelation 3:2).

A body that is dead does not respond. Stimulation simply does not affect it. When a body is alive it responds, acts, decides. Revival in the church presupposes that there is a living faith. Those Christian people had been alive, there had been a weakening of their faith until they did not respond any more to the things of God. When it is true of a person that once he believed the Bible and read it, but now he neglects it, soon his faith simply fades out. But there can be an arousing, there can be an awakening. This is the wonderful truth of revival. It is very common to think that when I am saved I have become different. And there is a sense in which that is partially true.

When the believer has been brought into fellowship with the Lord, one can expect different things from him as long as the Lord is having His way in him.

For example, the Christian life is a good deal as though you were seeking to row across a lake in a boat. You could row, or you could attach a motor and you would not have to row at all. The motor would push you across the lake easier and more rapidly. Or suppose you are in a building and want to go to the fifteenth floor. You could walk or ride an elevator. The motor in the boat or the elevator in the building did not change you. You were no stronger than before.

So when I think of myself becoming a Christian, I should not look into me to understand what happened. It is not that I am so different. When you find me doing differently, you should think of the Lord who makes the difference. Paul speaking of his experience wrote: "I am crucified with Christ: nevertheless I live; yet not I, but Christ liveth in me: and the life which I now live in the flesh I live by the faith of the Son of God, who loved me, and gave himself for me" (Galatians 2:20). The Apostle Paul recognized very well that it was the motor on the boat that put the boat across the lake. It was the elevator that lifted him up to the fifteenth floor. It was Christ living in him that made the difference.

The important thing about me as a Christian is my relationship with Christ Jesus. I know that part of it, part of my relationship with Him, is in my own hands, and that part I must seek to control and bring into His will. There are some things I can do. For instance, I can worship God. I can honor Him. I can turn myself around to look into the face of God. If I want the blessing of Christ, I could stop any day, any time in the day, and look up into His face. My hope is in Him. "My hope is built on nothing less than Jesus' blood and righteousness." So I look up, and worship God. The more I become impressed with His greatness, the more I become impressed with His strength, the stronger my faith becomes. "According to your faith, be it unto you."

Immediately following this, and probably right involved with it, is something that a good many of us will think of right away. And by the way we could come at it this way. One reason more people do not turn to God, and are inclined to stay away from Him and not look up into His face is the way they feel about their sin. But there is something they can do: they can repent! They can confess their sin.

I can bring myself into the daylight of His presence, the sunlight of the gospel of His truth! I can bring myself to turn to Him and confess my sin. By repenting I can come into the presence of God.

Another thing I can do is believe, not on me, not on what I'm going to do, not on what I promise to do, but believe on Christ Jesus who already has done it for me and is living now to do for me today and even more tomorrow. I can accept Christ Jesus as my Savior and Lord and also receive the Holy Spirit. I could do that any given day. I only need to say to Almighty God, "Let thy Spirit come in and take over as far as I'm concerned." If I do these things my faith will grow, and if my faith grows and is strong, Christ Jesus will work in me and I will have the blessing of God. So then let us "Be watchful and strengthen the things which remain and are ready to die."

58.

Current Emphasis on Spiritual Experience

Have you seen any signs among Christians today that encourage you to think believers are being blessed of God?

Then the priests the Levites arose and blessed the people: and their voice was heard, and their prayer came up to his holy dwelling place, even unto heaven (II Chronicles 30:27).

That is the way it happened in the Old Testament days when the people turned to God. I am often asked, "Are there any encouraging signs that would indicate that God is at work among His people today?" Yes! Let me say that we should not look for spectacular consequences all the time. When we talk about spiritual blessing we are tempted to tell only of the unusual, the spectacular, the tremendous; and of course, that's very natural. To see a giant oak fall to the ground is a notable event. To see that same oak tree grow through the years seems slow and simple and yet was not the growing the greater event? The falling itself was actually the lesser event. It made a bigger noise, took less time, but it certainly didn't have as good results as the growing. A house being on fire so that it's fully demolished is always far more impressive than that same house being built, being painted, being kept up. This truth is to be seen in spiritual things.

When we tell about conversion, we are inclined to select the dramatic instances. And so it often happens that those who have had a more simple experience wonder if they really belong to God, because they did not pass through some tremendous big shocking experience. Today world-wide evangelistic campaigns have been conducted with much effect. Also Inter-Varsity Christian Fellowship and Campus Crusade on college campuses reach thousands of students and college professors, who are committing themselves publicly to believing in the Lord Jesus Christ as their personal Savior. There are also groups such as Young Life that witness wonderfully to high school students.

Among the groups that deal with college youth is the Campus Crusade for Christ International, with its headquarters in Arrowhead Springs at San Bernardino in California. This is a tremendous affair. When I first went out there I could hardly believe my own eyes. They told me when I was getting ready to go that I would have as many as a thousand students in the first year classes. I appreciated their enthusiasm but I allowed for overstatement. I certainly did not expect to have as many as a thousand students. But the fact was that I taught each day over one thousand different college students about the gospel for four weeks. Each student attended class four hours each forenoon. In the afternoon he worked on his assignments. The professors gave them written assignments for each day and at the end of the four weeks a two-hour, written examination, which the student had to pass in order that he might get credit for that course. The students receive no money for being there. Those young people took five weeks out of their summer vacation and paid their own transportation, tuition and boarding expense. I was deeply impressed to see there eighteen hundred college students on one campus for five consecutive weeks, studying the gospel, learning about Jesus Christ. Why did they do this? The purpose of the training was to fit them to go back to their campuses, their four hundred colleges and universities in America, and tell about Jesus Christ to fellow students.

Also in our churches there are encouraging signs. First of all the practice of personal testimony. More and more in our churches we have instances of laymen who share in the order of public service to make a statement to the congregation of some aspect of their personal relationship to the Lord. We have young people getting up and testifying to the blessing that they have received from Christ, telling of their personal experience. In many churches there are special services. Sometimes we call them "Spiritual Enrichment," sometimes "Spiritual Emphasis." Also among our churches and throughout the congregations there is the distribution of booklets of testimony. Many booklets describing spiritual life are being circulated among the members while they think on these things. There are summer camps and conferences where young people and adults participate in learning about the gospel. Many of our churches have family schools of religion. That is a new idea, bringing the whole family to the church for several hours each day, in which the whole family thinks about the things of God. There are men's retreats and men's rallies, and young people's retreats and young people's rallies. There are cottage prayer meetings. People come for Bible study and for prayer. Many of our churches are beginning to have schools of missions. More and more in our churches, we give open invitation to people to stand up and confess Christ. There is a tendency to emphasize personal participation. God is working. He's working in the hearts of the people. We should never forget for one moment that Christ died for every single person, Almighty God wants to bring that soul to Him, regardless of the church, or regardless of the preacher, regardless of the officers, regardless of the program. Almighty God wants to bring that soul to Him, trusting in the Lord Jesus Christ and we thank God for His grace and mercy.

59.

Contemporary Demonstrations
of Spiritual Power

Do you think answers to prayer are real?

"All power is given unto me in heaven and in earth" (Matthew 28:18). Thus spake the Lord Jesus Christ. What an amazing statement! God through the Lord Jesus Christ is at work everywhere with power. It is important to remember that power can work silently and can work smoothly. Just think of the big trees in the woods. When you look up into the sky to see the tops of those trees can you realize there are tons of lumber in those trees? No human being ever arranged to put it there. Think of the power that is involved in those tons of wood there in the air. There is a similar situation in the spiritual world. God put those trees there quietly, silently, day and night, all year long. He put those trees there, and that is the way it happens in the spiritual world. The important vital working of the Holy Spirit can be quiet, unnoticed.

But on occasion works of wonder occur suddenly. Miracles happen and their testimony should not be overlooked. Among Christian people appear gifts of the Spirit. These can be seen primarily in such things as power in praying, speaking with tongues, healing by faith. There is a renewed interest today in the reality of the Holy Spirit of God and the gifts of the Spirit. Such phenomena are not superficial. Persons who have power in prayer and can cause results in answer to prayer, do not criticize the Bible. I have known many and have yet to meet one who questioned the Bible or ever doubted the things of the Lord. I am personally persuaded that the first immediate result of these events, that we call gifts of the Spirit, has been a renewed interest in and in many cases an actual confidence in the Holy Spirit of God.

There are also fruits of the Spirit: love, joy, peace, longsuffering, goodness, gentleness, meekness, self-control, faith. These are more important and more significant than the gifts written about in I Corinthians 12. Our generation has always had demonstrations of faith healing, as well as speaking in tongues. Throughout the history of the church, this has happened time and again and this speaking with tongues is not to be condemned. Paul himself said, "Forbid not to speak with tongues." Doubtless there are many sincere, genuine believers who share in this experience, but none of these gifts that are mentioned in I Corinthians 12 are essential to spiritual life. On the other hand, the fruits: love, joy, peace, longsuffering, etc. which are mentioned in Galatians 5:22 are always vital, always normal and always to be desired.

The Christian faces much in the world today that challenges his faith. Criticism of the Bible had undermined popular confidence, denominational and church formality has dampened the interest of well meaning people, power politics in church courts has stifled the working of the Holy Spirit among the brethren by ignoring the presence of the Holy Spirit and the power and purpose of the Holy Spirit. Just acting as if He were not to be thought about has deadened the spiritual life of many many congregations, and neglecting prayer has always smothered the response of the people who really would want to believe. In this sense Christians have been like sheep in the midst of wolves. In the meantime, popular skepticism has encouraged unbelief. Denial of the supernatural has discouraged faith. Confidence in man has blurred the gospel which involves depending upon Christ. Rejection of the claims of Christ has left men without hope. All that is true, but God has not left Himself without witness. In every congregation there will be some real, true believers in Christ, and there is an interest in the Bible. Interest in Bible study has increased in our day and time. Praying is being shared, and dependence on praying is growing.

I know of a group of ladies, older people, who call themselves the

Thursday Morning Prayer Group because that is what they are. They meet every Thursday morning and they pray. They pray for preachers. They pray for the radio ministry called "The Bible for You." They pray for the evangelical ministry of the gospel everywhere. These are not alone by any manner of means. Over the country as a whole, I don't think anybody has ever attempted to count how many thousands upon thousands of such groups there are who meet to pray and to promote the things of the Gospel and the preaching of the Word.

At the same time, among true believers, the presence of the Holy Spirit is being sought. There is more interest in the Holy Spirit, more actual trying to find out about Him and His work. There is more sale of books about the Holy Spirit. There are people who share with each other books of testimony about being blessed by the Holy Spirit. This is part of what the true believers are searching for. Personal witnessing is being studied. There are schools, institutes of personal witnessing, clinics held here and there over the country; people travel for hundreds of miles to go to some church where they can share in the training for personal witnessing. This is all going on in the world today.

I wish I could spread this before you as some big, tremendous, event that would be like a great noticeable thing, but that is not the way it happens. It is rather like the growing of a tree, a little here and a little there and as a result souls are being won, souls are being fed, and souls are being comforted. The evangelistic campaigns that you read about today are greater than anything in the history of the church. At the Inter-Varsity Conferences that met recently in Urbana, Illinois, thousands upon thousands upon thousands, as many as twelve thousand college students took time during their Christmas vacation to come to a central spot in our country where they spent days thinking about the things of the gospel. Nobody was paying them. They paid their way to go there, that they might learn about these things. The private studies that are going on all over are all indicating the interest that people have in the things of the Lord. Once again we can see God has not left Himself without witness. No matter how much you and I at one time may feel all alone, we are not alone by any manner of means. The Lord is with us. God is with us and lined up in His knowledge and in His wisdom are thousands upon thousands upon thousands of earnest hungry souls, seeking to glorify the Lord. And we pray that God will increase their number and bless them all for His Name's sake.

60.

How Can We Serve Him Best?

Do you have any ideas what a Christian could do today by way of really serving Jesus Christ?

> Brethren, I count not myself to have apprehended: but this one thing I do, forgetting those things which are behind, and reaching forth unto those things which are before, I press toward the mark for the prize of the high calling of God in Christ Jesus (Philippians 3:13-14).

As a human being I began as a natural man. And over all was God, whether I knew it or not. I was a sinner, guilty in the sight of God and certainly a sinner in my own self, interested in myself. Then came the Good News of the gospel to me. The Word came to me and finally was brought across to me that God so loved the world that He gave His only begotten Son, that whosoever believeth in Him should not perish but have everlasting life. And as I read that and studied it, I came to hear and read other sentences like this one: "In the fulness of time God sent forth his Son." And through all of my reading and my talking and my listening, I heard the joyful sound, "Jesus saves!" Suddenly I believed in Him and it was a glorious experience to be accepted in the beloved, received by Almighty God as His child. Since then I can tell you that so far as my spiritual life is concerned, I have never had a dull moment. In myself the old man wants to do as I please, but in the Spirit, in the new man, I want to please my Savior and my Lord.

Early in my spiritual experience, I learned to feed my faith with the sincere milk of the Word, and I thank God for the way in which I was interested in it. When I began to read and study the Word to see what it means really to believe in the Lord Jesus Christ, I found I was warned to beware of the devil. I was to resist him, for "he goeth about as a roaring lion seeking whom he may devour." And I was one of those he wanted to get under his control because I believed in Christ. Soon I learned a wonderful truth, the marvelous protection the Christian has in the Lord Jesus, through praying to Him. I learned to say with appreciation, "Satan trembles when he sees, the weakest saint upon his knees." It has always given me a sense of joy to know that in Christ I can be free from his power.

Also in my Bible study I learned the privilege and power of prayer. I found out that I could come into the presence of God not because I was good, and not because I was smart, not because I was strong, but because Christ Jesus died for me and I believed in Him. I rejoiced to realize the way was opened for me to come into the very presence of God. Also in the course of my studying the Bible I learned according to Scripture that I was a soldier of the King. I was called to be a good soldier for Jesus Christ and by way of being a soldier for Him, I learned I was not alone. I had comrades! There were other believers and I learned to appreciate them. Not only were there other believers, but I had a Companion, the Holy Spirit of God was given to be with me. And more than that, I have right now in the presence of God a Savior and a Lord. You have heard the song, "I have a Savior, He's pleading in Glory." That is just what He's doing. He is praying for me. And because of that I can have confidence in Him as I go about day by day. I have the Living Lord praying for me, I have the Living Holy Spirit walking with me, and I have the fellowship of other Christian people. Not only is all that true, but it is also true that the love of Christ constraineth me and I find in myself now an ambition: ambitious to be well pleasing in His sight.

I know the day in which I live is dark. I know that the clouds under which I live and move are heavy. I know that there is a storm threatening the whole world. I realize that spiritually there are many adversaries. But there are some things I can do. The Lord Himself said, "Be watchful and strengthen the things which remain, which are ready to die." To begin with I can worship. That's not hard. That's like a flower lifting up its face to the sun. You think it's hard for a dandelion to turn its face to the sun? That just comes naturally. Well I want to tell you right now that for a Christian it is just a natural thing to turn toward God and to lift up his heart to God. Any Christian can help himself that way. One way to do it simply is to go to church. I can go to God's House and be with God's people. In my congregation, and in my neighborhood there are people that believe in the Lord. I can be with them. And while I am doing that, I can also do more. I can honor the Lord's Day. I can make it a point that I am going to act on Sunday as if I were going to honor God. I can do that. If I honor Him, He will honor me. In addition to that, I can tithe my income. I can give to the Lord's work. I can make it a rule that I am going to give to the Lord's work. If I am not sure that I have given enough, I can double what I am giving. I will soon know how much I am supposed to give. The big thing is this—I must worship God. If I make a lot of Him, He will make a lot of me. If I look to Him, He will look after me. If I draw nigh unto Him, He will draw nigh unto me. I could not have it any better than that, because while I won't last down here forever, He lasts forever and ever and ever. When I put my trust in the Lord then I am safe and secure for all time and eternity.

There is also something I can do about the Bible. Since I have the Bible I can read it! To be sure I have read it before, but I have also drunk water before. I have eaten food before, too. So I can read it and honor it! I can treat it as if it were something important. I can be careful about it and study it. I can join other people who are studying the Bible. And then I can believe it. There are things I don't understand, things I don't know about for sure; but in my heart and mind I can believe it.

Another thing I can do is pray! Even if I have already done it, I can do it some more. If it has helped me, I can do it some more. Pray and pray and pray. I can remember what Paul told Timothy: "I will therefore that all men pray everywhere, lifting up holy hands, without wrath and doubting" (I Timothy 2:8).

I am discussing what I can do to serve Him. I am asking the question, How can I best serve Him? And I have noted that first of all, I can worship Him. In the second place, I can read His Word.

Now I am saying I can pray. And finally I can witness for Him. I can let it be known in my home that I believe in God. I can let it be known in my office that I believe in God. I can let it be known in my community that I believe in God. I can let it be known among all my friends that I believe in God. There is one way in which I can easily do that. Take a Bible with me. If I in my home keep the Bible handy and read it so that people can see me reading it, I am witnessing for the Lord. In the office, I can have a Bible with me, in my pocket, in my handbag, on my desk. Just the sight of a copy of the Scriptures is more than a flag! It will tell everybody in the community that I believe. If I am seen carrying a Bible, seen going to church, seen sharing in the things of the gospel, people will know in whom I believe.

I realize all this is so simple! I know it is a simple thing for an oak tree to grow. The tree does not make a lot of noise; it just grows. I can be that way as a Christian all the time. I can remember how the Lord said to me, "Repent and do the first works." If I continually start from the beginning and keep it fresh so that I walk with the Lord, God will bless me now and forever to the glory of His Name.